WITHDRAWN

Racial Discrimination
and Military Justice

Ronald W. Perry

The Praeger Special Studies program—utilizing the most modern and efficient book production techniques and a selective worldwide distribution network—makes available to the academic, government, and business communities significant, timely research in U.S. and international economic, social, and political development.

Racial Discrimination and Military Justice

Praeger Publishers   New York   Washington   London

PRAEGER SPECIAL STUDIES IN U.S. ECONOMIC, SOCIAL, AND POLITICAL ISSUES

Library of Congress Cataloging in Publication Data

Perry, Ronald W
    Racial discrimination and military justice.

    (Praeger special studies in U.S. economic, social,
and political issues)
    Bibliography: p. 85
    Includes index.
    1. Naval offenses—United States.   2. Race Discrimination—
United States.   3. United States. Navy—Afro-Americans.
4. United States. Marine Corps—Afro-Americans.   I. Title.
VB853. P47   359. 1'332   76-53541
ISBN 0-275-24180-7

PRAEGER PUBLISHERS
111 Fourth Avenue, New York, N.Y. 10003, U.S.A.

Published in the United States of America in 1977
by Praeger Publishers, Inc.

Printed in the United States of America

For Paula and Elizabeth

My Women of Valor

This study addresses the question of whether blacks and whites receive similar treatment in the criminal-justice system of the United States Navy and Marine Corps. The project arose in connection with the efforts of the Department of the Navy to obtain an objective assessment of the extent of racism in the sea services and its impact upon military life. The Office of Naval Research (contract number N00014-74-C-0456) provided the census of inmates in the navy and Marine Corps confinement facilities that forms the central part of this analysis. Battelle Memorial Institute's Human Affairs Research Centers in Seattle, Washington and the Institute for Social Research at the University of Hartford also provided technical support and facilities for the intensive secondary analysis of the data.

Essentially, the data examined here were drawn from a variety of official military records; much of the initial effort involved locating and bringing together existing data. Hence, much of the analytical focus is at the ecological level—upon aggregates of servicemen rather than upon individuals. We sought, by carefully examining these records, to detect evidence of any discriminatory policies or practices that might be operating within the criminal-justice system. Due to the nature of the data, certain kinds of evaluations were not possible. Notably, no attempt was made to characterize or assess prison conditions in the sea services or to evaluate the fairness of the Uniform Code of Military Justice. While these are interesting and important topics, it should be emphasized that they lie outside the scope of the present study. Instead, we have analyzed the consequences of the operation of the existing criminal-justice system and sought to determine whether or not blacks and whites are treated differently on an institutional level.

In addition to the prisoner census provided by the Office of Naval Research (ONR), a number of people helped in the acquisition of supportive data. Professor Johnnie Daniel of Howard University served as an able interpreter of the original prisoner census. Robert Guthrie and Eugene Gloye of the ONR served as valuable liaison people with the Department of Defense and as guides through the formidable federal bureaucracy. Robert Brandiwie of the Manpower Research and Data Analysis Center, Edmund Thomas of the Naval Personnel Research and Development Center, and Lt. Colonel Robert Moore from the Office of the Secretary of Defense were instrumental in the acquisition of data on the full personnel complement of the navy and Marine Corps. Without the able assistance of these men, the study could never have gotten under way.

A great scholarly debt is also owed to many colleagues who provided vital inputs and helped to improve the quality of the research. Dr. Carl A. Bennett, in addition to providing much of my statistical education, was the source of the idea for the study and oversaw the conduct of the analysis. Dr. Rodney Stark helped to shape the mass of data into a coherent manuscript and attempted to turn me into a sociologist in the process. My personal debt to these men, both for help with this study and in terms of my professional life, is much greater than I shall ever be able to repay.

Furthermore, Margaret Marini, Charles Moskos, and Paula Perry each managed to survive a detailed reading of the original manuscript, providing both professional criticisms and much-needed encouragement. William Anderson, Ernst A. T. Barth, David Gillespie, Robert Hayles, S. Frank Miyamoto, and Lynne Roberts also read selected chapters and provided useful commentary. Indeed, this study has benefited from the scrutiny of many fine professionals. It is my hope that the final product justifies their kindness and help.

CONTENTS

LIST OF TABLES

LIST OF FIGURES

Racial Discrimination and Military Justice

Especially since the violent racial incidents aboard the USS
Kitty Hawk and the USS Constellation in October and November of
1972, there has been widespread concern about racial injustice in
the sea services (that is, the U.S. Navy and Marine Corps). The
marauding bands of black sailors aboard the USS Kitty Hawk shouting
"kill the white trash" and "they are killing our brothers" (U.S.
Congress, House 1973, p. 17675) formed an incident that commanders
could not ignore. Indeed, it forced the Naval High Command to
acknowledge that at least some black sailors felt that discriminatory
practices existed in the sea services. This discovery was particularly
disturbing because for some time the chief of Naval Operations,
Admiral Elmo Zumwalt, had been moving to institute more fair,
liberal, and humanistic policies in the navy.

Following these incidents at sea, Mr. F. Edward Herbert,
then chairman of the House Armed Services Committee, commissioned a special subcommittee to study naval disciplinary problems.
The report of the special subcommittee concluded that there was
"no special evidence of racial discrimination . . . although certainly
there were many perceptions of discrimination by young blacks, who,
because of their sensitivity to real or fancied oppression, often enlist
with a 'chip on their shoulder'" (U.S. Congress, House 1973,
p. 17685). The special subcommittee, then, attempted to discount
real discrimination by citing a recent trend toward permissiveness
in the sea services and by suggesting that the perceptions of young
blacks formed an unreasonable basis for the uprisings.

This report was read with some suspicion by social-scientist
observers, who, among other things, worried that the formal inter-
views conducted by special congressional committees do not always
render an accurate picture of the situation. No specific charges of

calculated bias were made or intended, but it is well known among survey researchers that when high-ranking interviewers start their query with the top managers of an organization and move downward in the hierarchy, the subordinates are unlikely to refute the testimony of their superiors (Richardson, Dohrenwend, and Klein 1965, pp. 59-85). Knowledge of this difficulty, coupled with the fact that no body of objective data (for example, questionnaires or information from records) was collected, left the report of the special subcommittee vulnerable to several competing interpretations. As a consequence of these problems, the investigation and findings of the special subcommittee did relatively little to quell the controversy regarding racial injustice.

A major problem with the report of the special subcommittee, and of several other studies done at about the same time, is that the answer to the macro-sociological question "is there a real basis to discrimination" was assumed to be no, and the investigators then concentrated on the micro-sociological questions relating to men's perceptions. This is not to suggest that the micro questions should not be pursued but that the macro question must be answered first— as a prerequisite to map out which directions the micro analysis should take (see Stark 1975, pp. 25-46).

Hence, it becomes vital to determine whether or not there is an objective basis for the claims of differential treatment. The answer to this question has real policy implications that will determine the success of any proposed program (see Stark 1972, pp. 1-14). If real discrimination exists, the appropriate corrective must be to eliminate the sources of discrimination; nothing short of such a policy will provide the desired outcome. If there is no basis for real discrimination and, in fact, a problem of persons' perceptions of the situation exists, then a program emphasizing explanation of policies and education of servicemen is required. Attempts to eradicate discrimination when it does not exist or attempts to "explain away" actions that are clearly discriminatory will only produce heightened frustration and increase the probability of further outbreaks. Rodney Stark (1975, p. 8) rather succinctly outlines a logic that should form the basis of such policy-oriented research:

> Suppose that some ethnic or racial minority claimed that the courts needed massive reforms because they discriminate against that minority group. If it could be demonstrated that this group did not, in fact, receive discriminatory punishments for crimes and that for the same crimes their sentences were the same as those given to others, then the fact that they had a disproportionate number of their members in prison would most likely be discounted as a grievance.

The present investigation shall proceed following Stark's admoni-
tion, holding foremost the importance of careful controls and comparisons. Our research will center on the nature of the treatment
of blacks and whites involved in one aspect of the military criminal-
justice system: the prison population of the U.S. Navy and Marine
Corps. Prominent among charges of differential treatment of
servicemen based on race are claims of uneven application of military
discipline. Indeed, a study of perceived discrimination during basic
training reports that as weeks in training increase, members of
each racial group feel that the other group is getting more favorable
treatment (Thomas, Thomas, and Ward 1974, pp. 8-29). Our task
is to examine the basis for a component of real discrimination in
the prison system of the sea services. To this end, analyses will
be made of the relative compositions of the prisons and the services,
offense patterns and race, and sentencing practices.

As much as possible, the findings of this study will be integrated
into the body of knowledge already amassed by sociologists and
criminologists researching the civilian criminal-justice system.
Comparisons drawn between the civilian and military systems must
be examined with extreme caution for at least two reasons. First,
there is much less than unanimous agreement in the civilian literature
on arrest and sentencing differentials by race; this literature is
fraught with contradictory and inconclusive research reports (see
Stark and Cohen 1974, pp. 28-29; Terry 1967, pp. 219-20). Second,
and perhaps more important, are the basic differences between the
civilian and military criminal-justice systems that prohibit direct
comparisons (Skinner 1945, p. 8).

The first problem can be postponed for the moment—to be
discussed in the context of specific analyses to be presented later.
The second problem is more immediate and demands attention here.
Therefore, to guard against the drawing of misleading parallels and
to develop a feel for military justice and correction, the following
sections outline both the philosophy of correction and the military
criminal-justice system as they relate to the sea services.

PHILOSOPHY OF MILITARY CORRECTIONS

For centuries, discipline in the sea services was maintained
through threat of severe punishment for deviation. The naval charter
of England's King Richard I provided that "he who kills a man on
shipboard shall be bound to the dead man and thrown into the sea"
(Claver 1954). Other punishments included boring holes in the
offender's tongue, branding, and removal of the left ear with a sea
knife (Campbell 1813). Thus, for some time justice at sea repre-

sented one of the most systematically pursued deterrent programs ever implemented. It should also be noted that the program was reasonably effective, although brutal, as long as the size of the navy was small and most disciplinary actions were carried out aboard ship. Interestingly, under these circumstances punishments were administered swiftly and with considerable certainty, which, according to present-day psychologists, are probably the only circumstances under which a program of punishment is particularly efficient at maintaining order (Nuttin and Greenwald 1968).

Since the beginning of the twentieth century, the deterrent philosophy has begun to wane and in its place a trend to positive or corrective discipline has arisen (Janowitz 1960). The largest impact of the positive approach has been the elimination of the extreme punishments and the renaming of military confinement institutions. Guardhouses became stockades, chains in the hold became the brig, and the United States Naval Prison at Portsmouth Naval Base became the United States Naval Disciplinary Command. As Richard Henshel (1970, p. 29) describes the situation:

> the pervasiveness of that lip service [is] another symptom
> of the problem . . . . Everyone from the casual prisoner
> through the custodial personnel to the Confinement Officer
> and higher knows, for example, that punishment is a
> prominent feature of stockade existence, and that rehabili-
> tation as a programmed feature is virtually non-existent.

It should be noted, therefore, that while attempts are being made to implement rehabilitation philosophy and practice, a large part of being confined is simply "doing time." Personnel are not in a naval prison to correct a learning deficiency; they are there because, in spite of knowing what not to do, they did it. Also, in contrast to civilian as well as army and air-force prisoners, navy and Marine Corps prisoners must maintain the military regimen: They rise early, wear pressed uniforms, stand in formation, and march from place to place. In this fashion the line of military life is unbroken and the major life-style difference between sailors and imprisoned sailors is that those who are in prison are there for breach of rules and are thus denied certain gratifications (for example, liquor, sex, free movement, pay). Upon completion of sentence, most offenders rejoin their former units, performing the same tasks as before incarceration (Secretary of Defense 1975). In this sense, naval prisoners are fundamentally different from civilian prisoners— except for a temporary label of "prisoner," life on the inside is not terribly different from life on the outside. The exception to this rule is the style of work done by prisoners, which highlights the "programmed unpleasantness" aspect of naval confinement. To the radioman's mate, who may have a reasonable and stimulating job as a nonprisoner, the idea of spending one's work hours at hard physical labor or a very routine task cannot be attractive. Few military prisoners ever adjust to prison life so well that they come to prefer the inside to the outside. This is in contrast to some civilian prisoners who adapt to the prison regimen and social system and at least appear to fit into prison society much better than into the society at large. Keeping these basic differences of philosophy of correction and imprisonment in mind, we will briefly examine the actual structure of the naval criminal-justice system.

THE STRUCTURE OF MILITARY JUSTICE

Justice in all branches of the military derives from the Uniform Code of Military Justice provided for in the Constitution of the United States and in international law. The articles of the Uniform Code of Military Justice exist independently of federal, state, and local statutes and active-duty service personnel are always subject to the code; there can be no question of jurisdiction. The details of the military criminal-justice system are laid out in the Manual for Courts-Martial, United States. Herein are specified the types of military courts, their composition, the rights and obligations of accused and accuser, and the maximum punishments for those convicted of particular offenses. The following paragraphs sketch, in abbreviated form, the flow of military justice.

Military judges, attorneys, and courts (that is, juries) are always military personnel. Also, for the most part, members of the court are commissioned officers, although if an enlisted man is being tried, he may petition to have other enlisted men—superior to him in grade—form one-third of the court. Thus, military offenders are not tried by a jury of their peers. In fact, men of the same unit of the accused are not usually permitted to sit on the court.

There are three types of courts-martial: general, special, and summary. The courts are distinguished by their composition and by the maximum punishments they may impose upon a guilty offender. This latter feature also serves to limit the kinds of cases heard by particular courts. For example, murder cases may be heard only by General Courts-Martial, since they are the only courts that can impose death or a life sentence upon an offender.

General Courts-Martial are composed of a military judge and not less than five other members or, if requested by the defense, a military judge alone. Such courts can try any person in the armed forces for any offense specified under the Uniform Code of Military

Justice. Subject to the approval of the president of the United States, a General Court-Martial may pronounce any sentence specified in the Uniform Code, up to and including death. While these courts are usually convened only to hear more serious cases, any offender may request—and must be provided if he so requests—a General Court-Martial.

Special Courts-Martial are usually composed of a panel of not less than three members. Under special circumstances a military judge is assigned also, and when this is the case, the accused may petition to be tried by the military judge alone. Special Courts-Martial tend to be the workhorses of the military criminal-justice system, since they handle most of what are classified misdemeanors and lesser felony cases in the civilian world. Special Courts-Martial do not hear capital cases and cannot recommend that a member of the armed forces receive a dishonorable or bad-conduct discharge. The maximum punishment that a Special Court-Martial may impose is confinement for a period of six months or less or its equivalent (see Figure 1 for equivalent punishments).

Summary Courts-Martial are roughly the military equivalent of civilian justice courts. The court is composed of one member, always an officer. Summary Courts-Martial may only hear cases where the accused is an enlisted man and the maximum punishment such a court may impose is 45 days of confinement. Cases heard by Summary Courts-Martial tend to be minor and routine: common drunkenness, missing role call, disorderly conduct not related to performance of duty. Summary Courts-Martial have one additional unique feature in that there is the implicit requirement that the accused agrees that he is guilty and that the punishment meted out by the court is reasonable. This stems from the fact that, unlike the case for other types of courts-martial, the accused facing a Summary Court-Martial may initially request that his case be heard by a higher court or may request such a change of venue after hearing the verdict of the Summary Court-Martial. Such after-the-fact changes are not common, however, due both to the routine nature of the cases and to the fact that if a higher court hears the case and judges it guilty, it can impose a relatively more severe punishment. Figure 2 summarizes the relationships between the types of courts-martial.

Having taken the civilian-military differences in correctional philosophy and adjudication into account, we must mention one further qualifier with respect to military prisoners. This is the fact that a military offender may be discharged from the military as a consequence of conviction for a very serious offense; there is no civilian equivalent to this kind of punishment. Fortunately for the purposes of the present investigation, the impact of this procedure is not great.

FIGURE 1

Equivalent Punishments Established by the
Manual for Courts-Martial

Confinement on Bread and Water or Diminished Rations*	1/2 day
Confinement at Hard Labor	1 day
Hard Labor without Confinement	1-1/2 days
Confinement	2 days
Forfeiture	1 day's pay
Detention	1-1/2 day's pay

*Maximum authorized is three days.

Source: Adapted from Department of Defense 1969, pp. 25-29, sec. 127-C.

At least in the case of enlisted personnel, such discharges almost always become effective after whatever punishment imposed by the General Court-Martial has been served. Thus, discharges or demotions "effected under Article 58A are not a part of the sentence, but an administrative result thereof" (Department of Defense 1969, pp. 24-25, sec. 126f). A prisoner is discharged after serving his sentence; one cannot be sentenced to discharge.

The effect, then, of the discharge process on the population of military prisoners is almost nil for first offenders. There is an impact, however, with respect to "second-timers" or recidivists. If a person in a navy confinement facility has a previous military criminal record, we know immediately that his previous offenses were not serious ones; if they were he would not still be in the military. Thus, it becomes exceedingly difficult to characterize recidivists in naval confinement in the same fashion civilian recidivists are characterized. Usually, second-timers in civilian institutions are seen as the hard-core criminals: those who probably devote most of their outside activities to crime and those more likely to have long sentences. This is not the case in the sea services since such people are apt to be removed from the military. As a consequence of this situation, for all analyses that involve consideration of prior record, parallels to civilian data can be drawn only in the case of first offenders. The case of recidivists in military confinement is somewhat unique and of considerable interest in itself; our analyses of recidivists will therefore be performed separately.

FIGURE 2

Characteristics of Courts–Martial

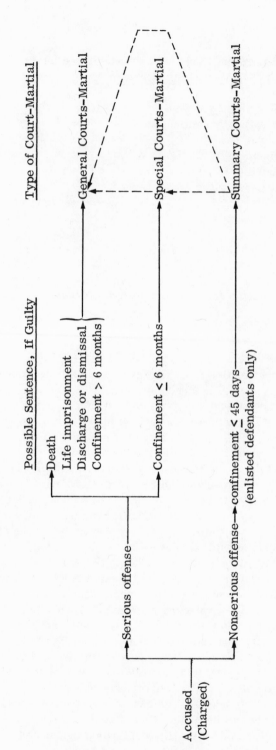

→ Represents normal route followed by offenders.

--→ Represents possible route by petition.

Source: Adapted from Department of Defense 1969, sec. 127.

THE DATA SOURCE

Given the aforementioned descriptions and qualifiers regarding criminal-justice practices in the navy and Marine Corps, consideration may turn to a description of the data that form the basis for the present investigation.

Toward the end of 1972, shortly after the incident aboard the USS Constellation, the Office of Naval Research began funding projects to gather data relevant to different aspects of the racial climate in the armed forces. The data to be analyzed here are a subset of data collected on military prisoners; specifically, we shall look at a census of enlisted-grade prisoners in naval and Marine Corps confinement institutions as of the last quarter of 1972.

The collection procedure involved a mailed survey. Confinement officers of all naval and Marine Corps prisons, stockades, and brigs were asked to respond to questions about their respective institutions and to provide an enumeration on selected characteristics of all prisoners being held at the time of the survey. As the project was sponsored by the Office of Naval Research, the response was virtually complete. All 13 Marine Corps institutions (see Figure 3) responded, yielding data on 1,626 incarcerated marines. Of the 30 naval institutions located worldwide, 27 (90 percent) responded with inmate data. Data were not received from the facilities at

FIGURE 3

Locations of Marine Corps Institutions
of Confinement

Supply Centers	Albany, Georgia
	Barstow, California
Bases	Okinawa, Ryukyu Islands
	Quantico, Virginia
	Camp LeJeune, North Carolina
	Camp Pendleton, California
Air Stations	Cherry Point, North Carolina
	Santa Anna, California
	Keneohe Bay, Hawaii
	Yuma, Arizona
	Iwakuni, Japan
Recruit Depots	San Diego, California
	Parris Island, South Carolina

Source: Compiled by the author.

FIGURE 4

Locations of Naval Institutions of Confinement

Stations	Adak, Alaska
	Keflavík, Iceland
	Long Beach, California
	Midway Islands
	Newport, Rhode Island
	San Diego, California
Bases	Brooklyn, New York
	Guantánamo Bay, Cuba
	Pearl Harbor, Hawaii
	Subic Bay, Philippines
	Key West, Florida
Supply Activity	Philadelphia, Pennsylvania
	Boston, Massachusetts
	San Juan, Puerto Rico
	Seattle, Washington
Submarine Bases	New London, Connecticut
	Charleston, South Carolina
	Guam
	Norfolk, Virginia
	Rota, Spain
	Treasure Island, California
Air Stations	Corpus Christi, Texas
	Dallas, Texas
	Jacksonville, Florida
	Memphis, Tennessee
	Pensacola, Florida
Fleet Activities	Sasebo, Japan
	Yokosuka, Japan
Disciplinary Command	Portsmouth, New Hampshire
Training Center	Great Lakes, Illinois

Source: Compiled by the author.

Brooklyn, New York; Midway Island; and San Juan, Puerto Rico
(see Figure 4). This shortage of three institutions is not problematic
in terms of the naval prisoner census because of two extenuating
circumstances: (1) the brigs at Midway Island and San Juan are small
and have maximum capacity of seven prisoners each, and (2) the
brig at Brooklyn has a capacity of 107 but has maintained an average
population size of 53 prisoners for the 1964-74 decade. Thus, most

of the total number of inmates are contained in the other 27 facilities.
It was estimated that if filled to normal capacity, the three missing
brigs would contribute 67 additional prisoners to the total (Peck 1975).
Since we have data on 881 incarcerated naval personnel, our census
represents 93 percent of the total prisoner population of the navy
during the last quarter of 1972. This number was deemed sufficient
to treat the navy data as if it were a full census.

For purposes of comparison, the census of inmates was supple-
mented by data on all navy and Marine Corps personnel not incarcerated during the last quarter of 1972. This information was
obtained through the Office of the Commandant of the Marine Corps,
the Office of Naval Research, and the Office of the Secretary of
Defense. Data on all types of discharges for the year 1972 were
obtained through the Naval Personnel Research and Development
Center, San Diego, California and the Office of Naval Research.
Thus, the full data set forms the basis for an excellent comparative
study of inmates and regular service personnel in addition to specific
analyses of the prisoner population.

PLAN OF ANALYSIS

One feature that will be prominent across all analyses is
description of the population. Since no previous multivariate
analyses of total prisoner populations are available, this descriptive
task is particularly important. All arguments regarding the prevalence of discrimination in the prison system of the sea services are
reduced to impressionistic speculation without such vital descriptive
data. The research questions investigated can be grouped into
questions relating to (1) the relative composition of the services
and the prisons, (2) offense patterns, and (3) length of sentence.

Recalling the previous discussion of whether racial incidents
were the function of perceived or real discrimination, we devoted
Chapter 2 to an examination of rates and proportions of types of
individuals incarcerated. Concern here is with answering the
questions of whether, in fact, blacks are overrepresented in the
prisons and with constructing a profile of incarcerated and nonincarcerated personnel, including examinations of race, educational level,
rank, and age. An analysis will also be made of discharge practices
and overall comparisons between the navy and Marine Corps will be
drawn. The goal of this chapter is to determine if and where discrimination exists.

Chapter 3 addresses the issue of offense and race. Attention
will be focused largely on the long-unresolved controversy regarding
the black violence hypothesis (see Stark 1973; Stark and Erlanger 1972).

From many civilian sources and for many years, social scientists
have observed that blacks are more often booked and convicted of
violent crimes than are whites. Much of these data, however, are
derived from bivariate analyses and have been called into question
because controls for social status have not been employed (Stark
and Cohen 1974; Stark and McEvoy 1970). Also, some attempts at
reassessing the offense-race relationship using social-status controls
have not resulted in the hypothesized disappearance of the correlation
(Davies 1970; Green 1970; Johnson 1941; Moses 1947; Pettigrew and
Spier 1962). It is generally argued, though, that if better measures
of socioeconomic status and life-style were available, the control
would destroy the offense-race relationship. The data at hand
provide an excellent opportunity to assess this claim. The military
is a sort of microcosm, noted for its bureaucratic tendency to treat
all creatures within certain categories in like fashion (Mandelbaum
1952). Thus, the lives of whites and blacks who have the same rank,
education, and age are likely to be quite similar; they receive the
same income, live in similar housing, and have similar demographic
characteristics. In this way, the measure of socioeconomic status
is considerably purer than corresponding measures in civilian
settings. If the argument that blacks and whites of the same social
status are equally likely to commit violent crimes is correct, a
control for social status on military-prisoner data will most certainly
bring the offense-race relationship to zero.

Finally, in Chapter 4 attention focuses on whether discrimination
in sentencing exists in the navy-Marine Corps prison data. In this
analysis, we are again faced with considerable disagreement in the
civilian literature regarding the extent to which blacks receive
discriminatory sentences. Early studies tend to report considerable
discrepancies in sentence length between black and white offenders,
even when controls for other important variables—social status,
offense, prior convictions—are used (Bullock 1961; Johnson 1941;
Sutherland and Cressey 1960, p. 266). More recent studies indicate
that when appropriate controls are employed, the race differential
does not exist (Green 1964; Stark and Cohen 1974; Terry 1967).
The discrepant nature of these findings is usually explained by noting
that the societal trend since the early 1960s has been toward racial
equality. This argument notwithstanding, there remains disagreement over the nature of the control variables required to destroy
any zero-order relationship between race and sentence length. On
the one hand, Stark and Cohen (1974) suggest that controls for type
of offense and prior record are sufficient to erase any race differences in length of sentence. The implication of this work is that
once the offender is "inside" the criminal-justice system, there is
a little discrimination based on ascriptive (that is, racial or social

status) factors. Discrimination by race or socioeconomic status is
seen as problematic primarily in the apprehension and arrest phases
of the justice system. Other researchers argue that age and socioeconomic status must also be controlled before sentence-length
differences between racial groups disappear (Green 1964; Terry 1967).
The present investigation, then, will document the existence or non-
existence of discriminatory sentencing and, if discrimination is found,
seek to determine the extent to which controls for different types of
nonracial variables mediate the race-sentence-length relationship
and the relative impact of different types of controls.

    The major findings of the study are summarized in Chapter 5,
which also includes a discussion of the implications of the present
research.

2

BLACK PARTICIPATION
IN THE SEA SERVICES

Blacks have served in the armed forces of the United States since the Revolutionary War (Lewis 1960). The history of black participation, however, reveals much variance in the conditions under which blacks have served, the nature of their service, and the rewards garnered from the society for which they served. Some of the variation is a function of differing policies among service branches regarding the treatment of blacks. Still more of the variation has been caused by the wax and wane of overt racism in the larger society which tends to be reflected in the military as a matter of official policy. Thus blacks in the military, no less than blacks in general, have been the objects of prejudice and discrimination–the idea that race and color form the basis for accord or denial of human rights.

For the military, at least, the practice of discrimination was officially proscribed on July 28, 1948. Executive Order 9981, signed by President Harry S. Truman, decreed that "there shall be equality and opportunity for all persons in the armed forces without regard to race, color, religion or national origin" (Department of the Army 1974, p. 24). Since the issuance of that order, not all racism has vanished from the services but the military has stayed in the forefront with respect to erasing the barriers of segregation and the inequalities of discrimination (see Northrup and Jenkins 1974).

Integration among the armed services actually began during World War II. It was prompted for the most part by military necessity rather than a desire for social reform. During this period the demand for soldiers and sailors was much greater than the supply available; there was tremendous pragmatic pressure to assign men based on their individual skills and expertise instead of their color. Faced with a "sink or integrate" decision, the military as a whole

14

opted for integration. President Truman's executive order, therefore, largely served to codify the already begun practice of integration
and to establish an official antidiscriminatory posture for the postwar
armed forces. As the following discussion will demonstrate, the
navy and Marine Corps have vigorously attempted to implement the
dictates of Executive Order 9981 through the creation of numerous
offices of equal opportunity, minority-relations programs, and special
minority-recruiting programs. It is interesting to note that in the
navy the roots of integration—albeit a peculiar kind of integration—
go back further than do those of segregation. The Marine Corps, on
the other hand, has a very different history.

BLACK PARTICIPATION IN THE NAVY

Blacks have served alongside whites in the American navy for
the past 200 years. Except for 20 years between 1922 and 1942,
black enlistments were always accepted by the navy. The range of
navy occupations or roles open to blacks, however, has fluctuated
considerably over the years. From the Revolutionary War through
the Spanish-American War, blacks were admitted in both combatant
and noncombatant capacities, and for the most part they filled
combat roles. Indeed, during the period from 1864 to 1898, the
United States awarded the congressional Medal of Honor to eight
black sailors for valor in action (Department of the Navy 1972;
Secretary of the Navy 1897). During the Spanish-American War,
John Jordan, a black chief gunner's mate aboard Admiral Dewey's
flagship the Olympia, fired the first shot at the enemy in the Battle
of Manila Bay (Mueller 1945, p. 11). Of particular note is black
participation in the Union navy during the Civil War: 25 percent of
the fleet was black (Department of Defense 1972, p. 95). The turn
of the twentieth century and the onset of the First World War, however, saw a decline in the availability of combat roles for black
sailors (Knox 1936).
    As the navy became more mechanized, ships became larger
and technologically more complex and blacks became less welcome
as and, perhaps, less technically prepared to be, sailors (Janowitz
and Little 1965, pp. 18-20). During this era, when blacks did enter
the navy, they served as messmen or stewards; at sea, they were
largely confined to below-deck duties. Still, there was no formal
ban on black enlistments and segregation was not pursued as a
systematic policy. Black stewards served white officers and in
this capacity also mingled with white sailors. Black messmen
usually worked as assistants to Filipino cooks who supervised a
racially mixed corps of sailors assigned the task of feeding the ship's

company (Duff and Arthur 1967, pp. 837-41). The racial diversity
of these sailors prohibited segregation, since messmen are quartered
and fed as a group. The fact that stewards are similarly quartered,
however, together with the fact that virtually all stewards were
either black or Filipino meant that some de facto segregation existed
for blacks in this occupational specialty.

Approximately 10,000 black Americans volunteered for service
in the navy during World War I (Northrup and Jenkins 1974, p. 24).
Most of these sailors, in keeping with the below-deck service practice,
were assigned noncombatant jobs, largely in the steward's branch.
Fully integrated crews were maintained aboard ship, however, until
1920. At that time, crew living quarters were segregated and
remained so until the beginning of the Second World War. It should
be pointed out, though, that the navy, unlike other services, has
rarely maintained fully segregated, deployable units. The equivalent
of the army's all-black regiment is largely absent from naval history
(Janowitz 1960).

In 1922, the navy officially closed its doors to blacks, although
men who had enlisted prior to that date were permitted to continue
their careers. A shortage of Filipino enlistments in 1936 brought
a partial reopening of enlistments when blacks were again recruited
for the messman's branch (Weil 1947, p. 96). The doors were
completely reopened on January 1, 1942, when World War II personnel shortages began to plague the navy. This marked the beginning
of the most recent era of black-white relations in the navy.

The pressures of a foreign war forbade the reinstitution of
segregation; there was neither money nor time to develop separate
living quarters for sailors, and gunners were needed more than
stewards. Hence, blacks entering the World War II navy, at least
officially, were trained and treated in a fashion quite similar to their
white counterparts. This is not to say, of course, that blacks did
not experience discrimination after 1942. System theorists in race
relations have pointed out that discrimination may occur at different
levels of abstraction: both individuals and organizations may dis-
criminate (Barth and Noel 1972, pp. 333-35). The present discussion
is meant only to suggest that institutional discrimination in the navy
sharply declined with the onset of World War II (Jones 1974) and that
this decline was strongly correlated with military requirements of
the time (that is, situational factors).

In 1944 blacks in general service were again being assigned to
duty aboard ship. Effectively, this move quashed all remnants of
institutionalized segregation in the navy—a practice which has not
reappeared. Integration has persisted through the Korean War, the
cold-war period in the late 1950s, and the Vietnam era. It is interesting to note that this policy has also survived pressures for change

from black sailors. Even when black consciousness ran very high
in the late 1960s, the navy rejected suggestions for segregated living
quarters for black sailors. Blacks are presently represented in
most professional specialties within the navy and, at least in terms
of official policy, face no closed doors to their career development
due to racial factors.

In summary, the American navy has progressed from an initial
period of open service for blacks, to a time of restricted entrance
at the turn of the century, through nearly 20 years of exclusion, to
the present-day policy of inclusion. The Marine Corps, discussed
in the following section, initially followed a policy of excluding blacks,
then developed segregated units during World War II, and finally
integrated after President Truman's executive order (Department of
the Navy 1968).

BLACK PARTICIPATION IN THE
MARINE CORPS

Black participation in the Marine Corps was introduced much
later than in the navy. The Marine Corps traces its origins to one
of two dates (Craige 1941, p. 66). The Continental Marines, largely
a small band of port guards, was formed November 10, 1775 by the
Continental Congress and disbanded after the close of the Revolutionary War. The United States Marine Corps was established by an act
of Congress on July 11, 1798. For the subsequent 144 years, the
marines did not accept black enlistments and very effectively maintained a policy of total exclusion.

In May 1942, the Marine Corps followed the lead of the navy
and began recruiting blacks to form a special battalion that became
the Eighth Field Depot—a unit that eventually won special commenda-
tions for action on Iwo Jima (Weil 1947, p. 96). From 1942 through
1948 the corps accepted black enlistments but maintained segregated
units for black marines, usually assigning them to supply or ammuni-
tion battalions. By the end of the war, 12 such all-black units had
been created (Lee 1966). At the time of demobilization (and shortly
after President Truman signed Executive Order 9981), all 12 of the
black units were disbanded and the blacks were integrated into other
existing units.

In the fall of 1949 the Marine Corps announced major modifica-
tions in its personnel policies with regard to blacks. The new
policies essentially permitted open enlistment of blacks for general
services in the Marine Corps with four limitations (Northrup and
Jenkins 1974, p. 30): (1) black officers could only be assigned to
units exclusively composed of black enlisted men; (2) black recruits

would be trained with white recruits on a nonsegregated basis; (3) black marines would be assigned to any unit where their particular military occupational specialty could be effectively used; and (4) black women marines were to be recruited for general service.

All restrictions on the conditions of service for black marines were lifted by 1952 and the color line was virtually erased by 1954 (Moskos 1966, p. 136). It has been pointed out that two major factors contributing to the fast and relatively smooth desegregation of the Marine Corps were its tradition of rigid adherence to orders and "the standard treatment—like Negroes—which is accorded to all enlisted personnel" (Moskos 1973, p. 98).

By the middle 1950s, then, both the navy and the Marine Corps were fully integrated and had implemented, for all practical purposes, the first official equal-opportunity plan for blacks in the history of American society. The period following the Korean War saw the beginning of the end of what has been called an era of "harmonious" race relations in the military (Stillman 1968). To a large extent a function of incidents in the larger society—the growing strength of the civil-rights movements, the passage of civil-rights legislation, a consciousness of kind among blacks—strains in black-white relations in the sea services began to develop (Nelson 1956). At present, blacks in the service, more boldly than before, are questioning and testing aspects of military life that appear to involve discriminatory practices. These actions are probably best characterized as tests of the flexibility and sincerity of the official policy of nondiscrimination. They represent efforts by blacks and others, both inside and outside the military, to secure and ensure their rights as Americans.

The following sections address the treatment of blacks within the prison systems of the navy and Marine Corps. Specifically we wish to determine the basic characteristics of military prisoners and assess the issue of black incarceration.

CONTACTS WITH THE CRIMINAL-JUSTICE SYSTEM

As the armed forces continued to reduce discriminatory practices, more blacks entered the services and remained to complete a military career. Table 1 indicates that the proportion of enlisted-grade blacks has increased from 7.5 percent of all enlisted personnel in 1949 to 12.1 percent in 1971. Similar increases are found for the sea services (see Table 2). The Marine Corps has experienced the largest and steadiest growth in black personnel, rising from 1.9 percent in 1949 to 10.7 percent in 1969. The navy, on the other hand, has increased slightly but in general has maintained a stable

TABLE 1

Black Composition of the Armed Forces

	1949	1965	1971
Total servicemen*	1,416,051	2,478,803	2,145,027
Total blacks	105,495	260,752	259,029
Percent black	7.5	10.5	12.1

*Enlisted-grade servicemen of the army, navy, air force, and Marine Corps.

Source: Adapted from Secretary of Defense 1975, p. 4.

proportion of blacks, hovering at just over 4 percent of all enlisted forces. In both services the increased number of blacks—blacks who had been guaranteed equal opportunity and access—introduced some interesting and heretofore unexperienced problems with traditional military institutions.

One of the first institutions to come under scrutiny was the military criminal justice system. Prior to 1950, the small number of blacks in the military and/or their second class status had all but precluded contact with military criminal justice. Often, when the accused was black, he was swiftly dealt with (sometimes on the spot) without any felt necessity for charges, trials, or incarceration (Knox 1936). Since blacks in the armed forces were emancipated, there has been a problem of ensuring equal treatment under the law. The first formal charges of racism in military justice were filed

TABLE 2

Blacks in the Navy and Marine Corps
(percent of total personnel)

Service	1949	1954	1962	1965	1967	1969
Navy	4.0	3.2	4.7	5.2	4.3	4.8
Marine Corps	1.9	5.9	7.0	8.3	9.6	10.7

Source: Adapted from Moskos 1973, p. 49.

during the Korean War (Department of Defense 1972, vol. 1, 102). These charges prompted a personal investigation by Thurgood Marshall, then serving as a special counsel to the National Association for the Advancement of Colored People. This investigation revealed some questionable practices; principally blacks were being booked and charged with crimes on little or no evidence. Although there is no doubt that blacks (as well as whites and others) were charged on scanty evidence which was later thrown from court, two particularly problematic aspects of the study make the finding almost impossible to interpret. First, the study examined only the cases of blacks; one is not given a sample of whites for comparative purposes. Second, the type of court-martial faced by the defendant was not specified. It is well known that Summary Courts-Martial are considered to be investigative in themselves and far more cases are routinely dismissed at this level than is the case with General Courts-Martial. Furthermore, Mr. Marshall did not separate courts-martial by service; an important consideration due to differing rates of court-martial between services. Thus, the Marshall investigation, like many that followed it, served more as a reminder that sustained scrutiny of the system is necessary to maintain equality than as proof of any inequity.

Courts-martial form the major point of entry into the military criminal-justice system and, as such, are of interest in the present analysis of prison composition. To develop a sensitivity for this particular avenue of entrance to the institutions under study here, we shall briefly assess the frequency of courts-martial, service differences in court-martial practices, and the outcomes of courts-martial.

For the fiscal year 1972, there were 21,139 courts-martial convened in the navy and Marine Corps. As Table 3 indicates, most of these courts were either special or summary, with General Courts-Martial (for major offenses only) accounting for 4.13 percent of the total. It is interesting to note that, overall, the Marine Corps convenes many more courts-martial than the navy. Collapsing across the types of courts, the navy holds 2.27 courts for each 1,000 of its enlisted personnel, while the marines convene 10.37 courts per 1,000 enlisted men. Furthermore, this differential holds within classes of court-martial; in fact the marine rate for Special and Summary Courts-Martial is more than four times that of the navy.

The outcomes of courts-martial suggest several interesting properties in addition to basic service differences. Table 4 presents a summary of the outcomes of all courts-martial convened during the period of June 5 through July 5, 1972, broken down by race and service. One immediately notices that acquitals and dismissals are rare outcomes for General Courts-Martial for both services. This

TABLE 3

Number of Courts-Martial Convened, Fiscal Year 1972

Service	General Courts-Martial Number	General Courts-Martial Rate per Thousand	Special Courts-Martial Number	Special Courts-Martial Rate per Thousand	Summary Courts-Martial Number	Summary Courts-Martial Rate per Thousand
Navy	203	.2	3,675	3.0	4,695	3.6
Marine Corps	670	1.8	5,755	14.5	6,141	14.8
Total	873	.9	9,430	8.8	10,836	9.0

Source: Adapted from Department of Defense 1972, vol. 1, p. 11.

TABLE 4

Outcomes of All Courts-Martial Convened, June 5–July 5, 1972, by Race and Service

	Navy White	Navy Black	Navy Total (All Races)	Marine Corps White	Marine Corps Black	Marine Corps Total (All Races)
General Courts-Martial						
Guilty	0	4	4	11	16	27
Not guilty	0	1	1	0	0	0
Dismissed	0	0	0	0	0	0
Special Courts-Martial						
Guilty	48	12	60	143	69	212
Not guilty	2	0	2	13	7	20
Dismissed	1	0	1	0	2	2
Summary Courts-Martial						
Guilty	10	1	11	74	31	105
Not guilty	5	0	5	9	6	15
Dismissed	0	0	0	1	0	1

Source: Adapted from Department of Defense 1972, vol. 3, pp. 179-276.

is no doubt a function of the fact that such courts are infrequently
convened and, when they are held, the offense is a serious one and
the case against the accused is usually well developed. Also, as
the Department of Defense (1972, vol. 3, p. 179) has noted, most
defendants appearing before a General Court-Martial enter a plea
of guilty.

Although there are some, the not-guilty and dismissed verdicts
are rare even in the lower courts. Of the 297 Special Courts-Martial
held, 29 or 9.76 percent were either judged not guilty or dismissed.
Similarly, 21 or 15.32 percent of the 137 Summary Courts-Martial
returned a verdict of not guilty or dismissed. One general point to
be made is that as one moves up in the hierarchy of courts, one is
less likely to obtain a verdict of not guilty or dismissed. There are
also service differences within the lower courts. For the 63 Special
Courts-Martial in the navy, 3 or 4.66 percent returned verdicts of
not guilty or dismissed. The Marine Corps held 234 such courts
during the same period and returned 26 (11.11 percent) not-guilty
or dismissed verdicts, a considerably higher proportion of releases
than the navy. This difference appears to reverse at the level of
Summary Courts-Martial with the navy releasing 5 or 31.25 percent
of the defendants and the marines releasing 16 or 13.21 percent of
its defendants. This apparent reversal between special and summary
courts is usually explained by making reference to variations in choice
patterns of defendants in the two services. It has been pointed out
that marines, given a choice, will usually ask for a Special Court-
Martial, reasoning that judgment pronounced by officers outside
their own company is at least somewhat preferred to maximize
objectivity (Erickson 1969, pp. 70-71). The navy, on the other
hand, is organized differently and the change from summary to
special court is usually only a change from one level of ships officers
to another level of ships officers (Locke et al. 1945, pp. 73-86);
hence, the perceived difference in objectivity between courts is low.
This explanation is supported when one combines the outcomes of
summary and special courts and finds that the navy released 8.86
percent and the marines 11.34 percent of its cases. Considering
the smaller number of Summary Courts- Martial in the navy, these
overall statistics are probably more stable estimates and do tend
to confirm that the conviction and release rates for the two services
are approximately the same.

The last question to be addressed with regard to courts-martial
is that of differential conviction rates between black and white
defendants. Table 5 is derived from Table 4 and shows the percent
judged guilty by service within racial groups and type of court.
Immediately, one sees that without regard to race, service, or
court, a high proportion of all defendants received the guilty verdict.

TABLE 5

Percent of Courts-Martial Judged Guilty,
June 5–July 5, 1972, by Race and Service

	Navy		Marine Corps	
	White	Black	White	Black
General Courts-Martial	0.00	80.00	100.00	100.00
Special Courts-Martial	94.12	100.00	91.67	88.46
Summary Courts-Martial	66.67	100.00	88.10	83.78

Source: Compiled by the author.

At the level of General Courts-Martial, this outcome is a virtual certainty in both services. In the two lower courts, the navy seems to return guilty verdicts slightly more often for blacks than for whites. The difference for Special Courts-Martial is smallest, with 94.12 percent of all whites tried being convicted and 100.00 percent of all blacks receiving a guilty verdict. The large difference occurs in the summary courts where two thirds of the whites and all of the blacks were judged guilty as charged. This difference, however, should not be interpreted as particularly alarming due to the small number of cases involved and the fact that the data represent only a one-twelfth sample of all cases. Taking these factors into account and paying attention to the outcomes for special courts, one may conclude that a minor race differential is present in navy courts with blacks being slightly more likely to be convicted than whites.

The Marine Corps produced equal (100.00 percent in each case) conviction rates for black and white defendants appearing before General Courts-Martial. Decisions of the lower courts, however, represent a change in direction from those observed for the navy. Although the difference is very small for each of the courts, the marines convicted a greater proportion of whites than blacks. For Special Courts-Martial, 91.67 percent of white defendants were judged guilty while 88.46 percent of the blacks were so pronounced. The difference is slightly greater for summary courts where 88.10 percent of whites and 83.78 percent of blacks were convicted.

To summarize, two facts should be kept in mind. First, the Marine Corps holds courts-martial more frequently than the navy and uses not-guilty and dismissed verdicts more often in the lower courts. Second, there are slight differences in conviction rates for blacks and whites between the two services; the navy pronounces the guilty verdict more often for blacks than whites and the marines convicts whites more often than blacks. As previously indicated, however, considering the low magnitude of the differences, a larger sample of cases would bring the conviction rates for blacks and whites more into line. The consequences of these points for our examination of incarcerated servicemen are twofold: whites and blacks have about an equal opportunity to be incarcerated as a function of a guilty verdict and marines, by virtue of the higher number of courts held, have a greater chance than navy personnel to be incarcerated.

The following section looks at prisoners versus nonincarcerated service personnel with respect to four background variables extracted from the criminology literature—race, education, income (pay grade), and age (Stark and Cohen 1974, p. 25; Terry 1967, p. 218; Wolfgang and Cohen 1970, p. 28).

PRISON COMPOSITION IN THE SEA SERVICES

During the last quarter of 1972, 881 sailors (.17 percent of enlisted-grade navy forces) and 1,626 marines (.92 percent of enlisted-grade marines) were confined in military brigs or correctional institutions. These figures yield incarceration rates of 1.74 per 1,000 enlisted persons for the navy and 9.16 per 1,000 for the Marine Corps. These data, then, suggest that the service differential found for courts-martial also holds for incarcerations: In general, marines are incarcerated at slightly more than five times the rate of naval personnel. To examine this observation and thereby scrutinize the apparent service differential, it is important to consider the characteristics of prisoners in the sea services. Who are these men in terms of their age, education, and pay grade and how do they compare with sailors and marines who are not incarcerated? It is known, for example, that civilian prisoners tend to be young, poor, and uneducated (see Dinitz and Reckless 1968; Clinard 1963; Cressey and Ward 1969; Knudten 1968; Savitz 1967; Schafer 1969). If this is also the case for military prisoners, and if it can be demonstrated that people with such characteristics differentially populate the two services in question, then we have taken a large step toward accounting for the service difference in incarceration rates.

Table 6 shows the distribution of navy and Marine Corps personnel and prisoners by age. A striking first observation is that as a body the Marine Corps is younger than the navy. Of all

TABLE 6

Navy and Marine Corps Personnel
and Prisoners by Age

	Enlisted Personnel		Prisoners	
	Number	Percent	Number	Percent
Navy				
17–19	96,850	19.17	378	42.91
20–21	112,634	22.30	294	33.37
22–23	87,517	17.32	106	12.03
24–25	45,948	9.10	44	4.99
26–30	58,200	11.52	21	2.38
31–35	57,514	11.39	10	1.14
36–40	33,161	6.56	2	.23
over 40	13,312	2.64	1	.11
Unknown	13	0.00	25	2.84
Total	505,149	100.00	881	100.00
Marine Corps				
17–19	56,249	31.69	630	38.75
20–21	53,097	29.91	577	35.49
22–23	24,883	14.02	296	18.20
24–25	11,601	6.54	74	4.55
26–30	11,738	6.61	34	2.09
31–35	9,264	5.22	3	.18
36–40	7,810	4.40	2	.12
over 40	2,837	1.60	1	.06
Unknown	15	.01	9	.56
Total	177,494	100.00	1,626	100.00

Source: Compiled by the author.

naval enlisted personnel, 41.47 percent are 21 years of age or younger, compared to 61.60 percent of all marines. At the other end of the age continuum, 20.59 percent of the navy and only 11.22 percent of the marines are 30 or more years old. Prisoners in both services tend also to be quite young. More than 76.28 percent of navy prisoners and 74.24 percent of Marine Corps prisoners are 21 or less. Virtually all prisoners—95.68 percent of the sailors and 99.08 percent of the marines—are under 30.

Prisoners, then, are proportionally younger than other enlisted personnel. This difference shows up particularly clearly when one looks at rates of incarceration for different age groupings. For the navy, men 21 and younger are incarcerated at a rate of 3.21 per 1,000 enlisted persons, while those over 21 have a rate of 0.71 per 1,000. Thus, men 21 and under are 4.52 times as likely to be incarcerated as those over 21.

This same age difference in the probability of incarceration is reflected in the Marine Corps. Marines 21 and younger are incarcerated at the rate of 11.04 per 1,000 enlisted men. The rate for those over 21 declines to 6.15 per 1,000, revealing that younger marines are nearly twice as likely to be incarcerated.

The between-service differences in rates for the age groups are also great. A marine 21 or under is 3.44 times as likely to be incarcerated as a sailor of the same age. Marines over 21 are 8.66 times more likely to be imprisoned than navy personnel over 21. Thus, the Marine Corps is less hesitant than the navy to imprison older members of the service. What this last difference emphasizes is the greater relative importance of age as a factor in incarceration for the navy than for the marines.

The services differ at least as much with respect to education as they do by age. Personnel in the navy are generally more educated than personnel in the Marine Corps (see Table 7). A high-school diploma or its equivalent is held by 77.09 percent of naval enlisted personnel, while 57.36 percent of all marines are high-school graduates. Among enlisted men of both services, education beyond high school is rare; 8.52 percent of the sailors and 7.33 percent of the marines fall into this category. Indeed, most military enlisted personnel have not attended college. The presence of post-high-school educated people in these data is largely accounted for by the military draft which was still operating in 1972 and by the fact that student deferments were lifted in late 1970 (Janowitz 1975).

Once again, prisoners in both services tend to be less educated than their nonincarcerated counterparts. As Table 7 shows, nearly 50 percent of all naval prisoners have not completed high school. Furthermore, the incarceration rate for those who have less than a high-school education is 6.01 per 1,000 enlisted men; a rate 5.83 times higher than the 1.03 per 1,000 that holds for those with a high-school diploma or more.

The pattern for the Marine Corps is even more pronounced. Marine prisoners with less than a high-school education account for 67.34 percent of all incarcerated personnel. Overall, this education group has an incarceration rate of 18.18 per 1,000 enlisted men. This is considerably higher than the 4.53 per 1,000 for marines with a high-school diploma or more, who constitute only 32.66 percent of the prisoners. Thus, a marine without a high-school education is 4.01 times as likely to be incarcerated as one with a high-school diploma.

TABLE 7

Navy and Marine Corps Personnel and
Prisoners by Education

	Enlisted Personnel		Prisoners	
	Number	Percent	Number	Percent
Navy				
Less than high school	72,696	14.39	437	49.60
High-school diploma or GED*	389,435	77.09	391	44.38
Some college or vocational school	35,509	7.03	46	5.22
College graduate	7,358	1.46	0	0.00
Graduate school	151	.03	0	0.00
Unknown	0	0.00	7	.80
Total	505,149	100.00	881	100.00
Marine Corps				
Less than high school	60,245	33.94	1,095	67.34
High-school diploma or GED*	101,815	57.36	470	28.91
Some college or vocational school	12,101	6.82	53	3.26
College graduate	836	.47	1	.06
Graduate school	65	.04	1	.06
Unknown	2,432	1.37	6	.37
Total	177,494	100.00	1,626	100.00

*General Equivalency Degree
Source: Compiled by the author.

Turning attention to service comparisons, the higher incarceration rates that prevail in the Marine Corps are once again evident. A marine with a less than high-school education is 3.02 times more likely to be incarcerated than his counterpart in the navy. Marines who have finished high school or gone further are 4.40 times as likely to be incarcerated as naval enlisted personnel with a similar education. Although it is known that the Marine Corps is generally harsher than the navy in matters of discipline (see Briggs 1958; Brodsky and Komaridis 1966 and 1968; Canter and Canter 1957; Chappell 1945; French and Ernest 1955), the difference in basic task structure between the two services also slightly inflates the discrepancy in incarceration rates. The more technical nature of

most jobs in the navy requires that sailors have more education.
Also, while the navy has long had a policy that encourages enlistees
to have a high-school diploma, the Marine Corps only recently adopted
such a policy. As a consequence, the navy has proportionately more
high-education people—who in turn have lower incarceration rates—
than the Marine Corps.

The principle of hierarchy is pervasive in the military and
perhaps the hallmark of hierarchy is represented by the pay grade
(rank) system among enlisted personnel. It should be pointed out
that one's pay grade (E1—lowest—through E9—highest) is a very good
estimate of income as well as level of responsibility and will be used
here as such.

It is almost an axiom that the higher the pay grade (rank), the
lower the probability of incarceration. In the navy, 70.38 percent
of all prisoners are in the two lowest pay grades (see Table 8). The
rate of incarceration for E1- and E2-level sailors is 6.06 per 1,000
or 9.47 times the rate for all grades E3 and above (which equals
0.64 incarcerations per 1,000 enlisted men).

Among Marine Corps prisoners, 86.59 percent occupy the two
lowest pay grades. Marines who rank either E1 or E2 have an
incarceration rate of 18.94 per 1,000; 9.11 times higher than the
rate of 2.08 for higher-ranking marines and 3.13 times greater than
the rate for sailors ranking E1 or E2. When one considers that
92.63 percent of navy and 94.89 percent of marine prisoners rank
E3 (seaman or lance corporal) or below, the accuracy of the previously mentioned axiom becomes rather clear. Indeed, the fact of
low rank is virtually a constant for prisoners in the sea services.

To this point we have constructed a portrait of the military
prisoner on the whole as young (21 years old or less), with less than
a high-school education, and occupying the lower pay grades. It has
also been noted that part of the navy-Marine Corps incarceration-
rate differential is a function of the disproportionately high number
of individuals who match these characteristics in the Marine Corps.
Thus, the navy incarcerates fewer people but has, on the average,
older and more highly educated personnel than the marines.

The final question to be addressed in this section relates to
race and incarceration. Given this analysis of the characteristics
of military prisoners in general, where do blacks fit into the scheme?

In the last quarter of 1972, there were 36,838 black enlisted
men in the navy (who accounted for 7.29 percent of all enlisted
personnel). The marines, on the other hand, had proportionately
more than twice as many blacks: almost 16 percent of the enlisted
forces (see Table 9).

In the navy, blacks are heavily overrepresented in the prisoner
population. While only 7.29 percent of the enlisted personnel are

TABLE 8

Navy and Marine Corps Personnel and
Prisoners by Pay Grade

	Enlisted Personnel		Prisoners	
	Number	Percent	Number	Percent
Navy				
E7–E9	50,156	9.90	0	0.00
E6	72,932	14.60	1	.11
E5	87,866	17.40	13	1.48
E4	105,247	20.80	47	5.33
E3	85,717	17.00	196	22.25
E2	69,981	13.90	273	30.99
E1	32,250	6.40	347	39.39
Unknown	0	0.00	4	.45
Total	505,149	100.00	881	100.00
Marine Corps				
E7–E9	13,555	7.60	2	.12
E6	12,420	7.00	2	.12
E5	25,350	14.30	24	1.48
E4	22,509	12.70	52	3.20
E3	29,310	16.50	135	8.30
E2	35,192	19.80	294	18.08
E1	39,158	22.10	1,114	68.51
Unknown	0	0.00	3	.18
Total	177,494	100.00	1,626	100.00

Source: Compiled by the author.

black, nearly 20 percent of the prisoners are from this racial group.
Furthermore, the incarceration rate for white enlisted men in the
navy is 1.49 per 1,000, compared with 4.70 per 1,000 for blacks.
Navy blacks, relative to whites, are therefore 3.15 times more
likely to be incarcerated.

Interestingly, the racial pattern for the Marine Corps is quite
different. First, blacks are only somewhat overrepresented in the
Marine Corps prisons: 23.80 percent of prisoners and 15.80 percent
of all personnel are black. Blacks, however, are incarcerated at
a rate of 13.80 per 1,000, while the rate for whites is 7.95 per 1,000.
The important point here is that among marines, the rate for blacks
is only 1.74 times higher than the rate for whites. Comparing the

TABLE 9

Navy and Marine Corps Personnel and
Prisoners by Race

	Enlisted Personnel		Prisoners	
	Number	Percent	Number	Percent
Navy				
White	443,777	87.85	662	75.14
Black	36,838	7.29	173	19.64
Other	24,534	4.86	44	4.99
Unknown	0	0.00	2	.23
Total	505,149	100.00	881	100.00
Marine Corps				
White	146,329	82.44	1,164	71.59
Black	28,044	15.80	387	23.80
Other	2,449	1.38	75	4.61
Unknown	672	.38	0	0.00
Total	177,494	100.00	1,626	100.00

Source: Compiled by the author.

two services, we find that the navy's black-white arrest differential
is nearly twice as big as the differential for the Marine Corps.
While any marine is more likely to be imprisoned than a sailor,
the incarceration rate for black marines relative to whites is considerably lower than the comparable rate for the navy. Therefore,
we begin our examination of race and incarceration by observing
that blacks are overrepresented in the prison populations of both
sea services but much more overrepresented in the navy.

The demographic characteristics of enlisted-grade blacks in
the navy approximate those outlined previously as generally repre-
sentative of incarcerated populations. Twenty-four percent of the
blacks, as compared with 13 percent of the whites, lack a high-
school education. There are also more young blacks (53.77 percent
are 21 or less) than young whites (41.98 percent are 17-21 years
old), and blacks are disproportionately represented in the lower pay
grades (57.38 percent of blacks and 33.47 percent of whites fall into
the three pay categories E1-E3).

Table 10 cross classifies navy personnel and prisoners by age,
education, and race. As expected, we notice that among all enlisted
personnel there are proportionately more blacks than whites in the

TABLE 10

Navy Personnel and Prisoners by Age, Education, and Race

Age	Education	Enlisted Personnel				Prisoners			
		White		Black		White		Black	
		Number	Percent	Number	Percent	Number	Percent	Number	Percent
17–21	Less than high school	36,107	8.14	5,592	15.18	292	45.48	66	39.29
	High school graduate	147,083	33.15	14,079	38.22	202	31.46	67	39.88
	Beyond high school	3,105	.70	137	.37	17	2.65	4	2.38
22–27	Less than high school	8,113	1.83	870	2.36	35	5.45	9	5.36
	High school graduate	112,825	25.43	5,864	15.92	71	11.06	14	8.33
	Beyond high school	25,031	5.64	638	1.73	12	1.87	4	2.38
28 and over	Less than high school	15,698	3.54	2,155	5.85	5	.78	2	1.19
	High school graduate	84,411	19.02	6,907	18.75	8	1.25	2	1.19
	Beyond high school	11,334	2.55	596	1.62	0	0.00	0	0.00
Total		443,707	100.00	36,838	100.00	642	100.00	168	100.00

Source: Compiled by the author.

17-21 age group, and across all age groups there are more blacks than whites in the less-than-high-school-education category. This difference is particularly evident among 17-21 year olds without a high-school diploma: there is nearly twice the proportion of blacks in this category as whites. Blacks and whites in the prisoner population, however, show much more homogeneity with respect to age and education.

Nearly 80 percent of the navy's prisoners are white and about 20 percent are black. Among prisoners, 79.59 percent of the whites and 81.55 percent of the blacks are aged 17-21 years. Thus there is virtually no difference between black and white prisoners with regard to age group. There is a slightly greater difference on the education dimension, with 51.71 percent of the white prisoners and 45.84 percent of the black prisoners lacking the high-school diploma.

When we examine the percentage columns for prisoners in Table 10, it becomes apparent that, for blacks, age is a more important variable with respect to incarceration than educational levels. While the proportion of less- to greater-than-high-school-educated blacks is fairly constant across age categories, the 17-21-year-old group contains a much greater proportion of black prisoners than either of the other two age categories. Therefore, in explaining black incarcerations, presence in the 17-21 age category—without regard to gross level of education—significantly increases the chances of imprisonment.

The age pattern for white prisoners is similar to that for blacks: the greatest proportion is in the youngest age grouping. Thus, there is a definite main effect of age for whites, too, with the highest incarceration rate in the 17-21-year-old group. Unlike blacks in the lower age group, though, whites show a distinct effect for education. Almost 80 percent (511 men) of the white prisoners are in the 17-21 age category. Of these prisoners, 57.14 percent lack a high-school diploma and 42.86 percent are either high-school graduates or have gone beyond. Among whites in the lowest age group, then, as education increases the proportion of whites incarcerated decreases.

To summarize, most naval prisoners, whether black or white, are 17-21 years old. For blacks, the age factor is most prominent with education (less than high school versus high school or more) not having a big impact. For white prisoners, both age and education are reflected in incarceration—the proportion of incarcerated 17-21 year olds declining with increasing education.

Prisoners in the Marine Corps rather closely approximate the age, education, and race proportions of naval prisoners. The majority of all prisoners (77.29 percent of whites and 67.01 percent of blacks) fall into the 17-21-year-old age group. Furthermore,

TABLE 11

Marine Corps Personnel and Prisoners by Age, Education, and Race

| Age | Education | Enlisted Personnel | | | | Prisoners | | | |
| | | White | | Black | | White | | Black | |
		Number	Percent	Number	Percent	Number	Percent	Number	Percent
17–21	Less than high school	40,467	27.36	9,876	33.21	672	58.23	171	44.76
	High school graduate	47,240	31.94	9,196	30.93	209	18.11	78	20.42
	Beyond high school	3,454	2.34	589	1.98	11	.95	7	1.83
22–27	Less than high school	6,749	4.56	1,838	6.18	132	11.44	56	14.66
	High school graduate	21,980	14.86	4,031	13.56	103	8.93	52	13.61
	Beyond high school	6,158	4.16	793	2.67	18	1.56	16	4.19
28 and over	Less than high school	3,194	2.16	672	2.26	5	.43	0	0.00
	High school graduate	16,320	11.03	2,477	8.33	4	.35	2	.52
	Beyond high school	2,357	1.59	263	.88	0	0.00	0	0.00
Total		147,919	100.00	29,735	100.00	1,154	100.00	382	100.00

Source: Compiled by the author.

33

among both black and white marines, there is a pronounced education effect with regard to the proportion incarcerated across age groups. As the percentage columns for black and white prisoners in Table 11 indicate, the proportion of marines incarcerated at each age level declines as we move from the less-than-high-school category to high-school graduates or more. The decline is most pronounced for all white age groups and for blacks 17-21 years and less pronounced, although still noticeable, among older blacks.

The proportional distinctions of black and white prisoners in both services is, therefore, quite similar: Prisoners tend to be drawn from the youngest age groups and lowest educational groups. In an effort to introduce an analytic and comparative flavor, one can examine rates of incarceration, rather than prisoner proportions, while introducing pay grade (rank) into the scheme. Thus, the closing section summarizes black-white differences in incarceration rates and compares the navy and Marine Corps with regard to their treatment of blacks.

RACE AND INCARCERATION: SUMMARY
AND CONCLUSIONS

Table 12 shows incarceration rates per 1,000 enlisted men for blacks and whites in the navy and Marine Corps by age, education, and pay grade. Beginning with the navy, these rates permit comparisons of the relative plight of blacks and whites and facilitate the identification of patterns in incarceration.

As previously noted, most navy prisoners fall into the E1-E3 range of pay grades; due to a lack of cases in the E4-E9 range, the emphasis in the naval analyses will be on patterns in the lower ranks. There are two prominent patterns for both blacks and whites in the navy. First, as education increases, the absolute rate of incarceration decreases. Second, as age increases the incarceration rate for sailors in the lower enlisted ranks increases by a factor of about 1.5 times (for both educational levels).

Among sailors with less than a high-school education, the black incarceration rate is only slightly higher than the white rate, for all age groupings. Blacks in the 17-21 age group have a rate 1.39 times higher than whites; for the 22-27 year olds, the black rate is 1.52 times the white rate. Therefore, in the low-education category, black and white incarceration rates are only slightly out of line with one another. For personnel with a high-school diploma or more, however, there exists a considerable discrepancy between black and white rates. Although the rates themselves are lower than the rates for personnel lacking a high-school diploma, blacks at this

TABLE 12

Incarcerated Personnel by Service, Race,
Education, Age, and Rank
(per thousand enlisted men)

Rank	Age	Education	Navy		Marine Corps	
			White	Black	White	Black
E1–E3	17–21	Less than high school	8.72	12.15	18.55	17.77
		High school or more	2.00	5.47	5.56	9.69
	22–27	Less than high school	13.23	20.13	40.24	43.34
		High school or more	3.16	6.87	15.27	29.60
	28 and over	Less than high school	–*	25.00	–	–
		High school or more	6.13	22.24	9.10	⊥
E4–E9	17–21	Less than high school	.22	–	3.13	7.08
		High school or more	.31	–	.64	–
	22–27	Less than high school	.86	–	2.94	3.38
		High school or more	.11	–	.97	2.53
	28 and over	Less than high school	.32	–	1.30	–
		High school or more	.04	–	.10	–

*Too few prisoners for meaningful estimate of rate.
Source: Compiled by the author.

level are more than two times as likely to be imprisoned as whites.
This is true across age groups where 17–21-year-old blacks have
a rate 2.74 times that for whites, the rate for 22–27-year-old blacks
is 2.17 times bigger than the white rate, and blacks 28 years and
older are 3.63 times more likely than whites to be imprisoned. Thus,
while blacks and whites in the lowest educational categories are treated

at least similarly, there is considerable particularism in the navy with respect to the incarceration of black and white personnel with a high-school education or more. Navy blacks in the upper educational grouping have a disproportionately high incarceration rate even when age is taken into account.

Among Marine Corps personnel, like the navy, incarceration rates are highest for men in the E1-E3 pay grades. As pointed out previously, however, the incarceration of E4-E9 personnel is a much more common practice in the marines than in the navy; hence, Table 12 does show marine incarceration rates for personnel in the higher pay grades. It should be noted that rates for E4-E9-level personnel in the marines follow different patterns from those in the lower ranks and are considerably lower in absolute magnitude. One common pattern across both rank categories, however, is the decline in incarceration rate as education increases. This pattern holds across age categories for both blacks and whites.

Within categories of education, the incarceration rate for both blacks and whites drastically increases with age in the E1-E3 pay group. Charles Moskos (1970, pp. 4-13), in a recent analysis of enlisted men, has rather nicely characterized the situation by commenting that from the authorities' point of view, the only creature more annoying than a young, low-ranking, problem soldier is an old, low-ranking, problem soldier. In fact, the increasing incarceration rate with age in this rank category is not particularly surprising when it is considered that "getting into trouble" often keeps these men in the lower ranks, and the more frequently one has clashes with the rules, the longer one stays at the bottom of the rank structure. The reversal of this relationship in the E4-E9 rank category, where incarceration rate consistently declines with increasing age for both racial groups, tends to strengthen the postulated explanation.

Like the navy, black and white marines in the E1-E3 rank category with less than a high-school education have very similar incarceration rates. Although the absolute rate increases with age, the increase is about the same for blacks as for whites. Thus, for 17-21-year-old, E1-E3 marines, the black incarceration rate is .96 times the white rate and for the 22-27 age group the black rate is 1.08 times the white rate. Not only is the differential very small, but the absolute size of the Marine Corps black-white difference is much smaller than the case for the navy—a finding that indicates that at this rank and educational level, the marines are less discriminating than the navy. For the E4-E9 rank group, the black-white differential among marines with less than a high-school education is larger than in the lower ranks but declines beyond the youngest age category to a comparable and more tolerable level.

For personnel with a high-school education or more, the marine black-white differential in incarceration rates is larger than was the case for the lowest educational grouping. Blacks with a greater-than-high-school education in the E1-E3 group are 1.74 times as likely to be incarcerated as whites in the 17-21 age group and 1.94 times more likely in the 22-27-year-old group. The marines, therefore, reflect the same discrepancy found for the navy but to a smaller degree.

In summary, some discrepancies in black-white incarceration rates are present in both services but of smaller magnitude in the Marine Corps than in the navy. In both cases, the problem is with a very high relative incarceration rate for blacks with a high-school education who are older and still on the bottom of the rank structure. It should be emphasized that in the military a person—whether black or white—with these demographic characteristics is a problem. Such a person is faced with an almost inescapably difficult set of life circumstances: (1) he is probably supervised by people with lower education who are younger than himself; and (2) previous scrapes with rules have prevented his promotion and labeled him a "problem soldier." These circumstances virtually guarantee that his stress and frustration levels will remain high and that he will be carefully watched and probably prosecuted even for small infractions of the rules. These conditions would apply to both blacks and whites.

The question of why the black rate is not only high but higher than that for whites may be addressed in terms of comparative opportunities for such people outside the military. This should be considered since the obvious answer to the problem of high stress and frustration is to leave the service at one's first opportunity. For whites with a high-school diploma who are 22 or older, the employment opportunities in the civilian world are not bad. Indeed, it would not be hard for a white to find a position on the outside with a better income and equal security without the stress and frustration in the military. The necessary factor for whites to escape the "problem category" is the energy to make the move.

In 1972 and to some extent now, blacks over 22 with a high-school diploma faced a different problem. Overt racial discrimination was higher in the civilian world anyway, and there was no particular guarantee that a secure and equally well-paying job could be found on the outside. Thus, the frustration in the civilian setting was at least as high and chances were good that the work would be equally displeasurable, lower paying, and less reliable. With a choice like that, even a person of questionable rationality would opt for the military. And, apparently, many such blacks have stayed in and are incarcerated more frequently, resulting in the higher rates witnessed here.

The competing explanation for the concentration of blacks in the lower-rank, higher-education, older-age-group category centers around the idea that blacks are not promoted at the same rate as whites—that is, blacks are discriminated against by a promotion policy that denies them advancement. The major factor mediating against this explanation is the promotion process itself. For both the navy and the Marine Corps, recruits are awarded the rank of E1 upon enlistment and advanced to E2 upon completion of basic training. Further promotions are a function of four factors: (1) the appropriate amount of time in grade, (2) the serviceman's performance on a written examination or in a training school, (3) the recommendation of his immediate superior, and (4) his service record to date. In both services, greatest emphasis is placed on examination perform- ance (Northrup and Jenkins 1974, p. 188); it would be difficult to be an E5 radioman's mate and effectively execute the supervisory responsibilities of that office if one did not thoroughly understand the technology of electronics. It should be noted that this emphasis on technological expertise as a prerequisite for promotion has come to be emphasized only since the 1940s but nevertheless now plays a significant role in advancement.

When one considers that the examinations are standardized service-wide and graded in a central processing center (usually not on the same base as the serviceman who took the exam), it becomes clear that particularism (discrimination) in scoring the exams is probably nonexistent. Furthermore, the scheduling of promotion examinations is largely automatic. When the serviceman's time-in-grade requirement is filled, he is notified and scheduled for examination; one need not obtain permission to take an examination for advancement.

Therefore, given that the examining procedure is open and subject to little particularism, we can consider why a serviceman would be blocked from promotion. Once time in grade is met and the examination has been taken, the major factor resulting in failure to be promoted is failing the exam. Among servicemen who have passed the examination, most are promoted (Northrup and Jenkins 1974, p. 198); those who are not advanced at this stage are usually servicemen with recent criminal records who do not have a favorable report from their immediate superiors. It is interesting to note that men with an offense more than a year old and no subsequent offenses are usually promoted if their exam performance is adequate (Henshel 1970, p. 142). The purpose of this discussion has been to emphasize that especially in the last 20 years, the promotion pro- cedures in the sea services have become systematized and bureau- cratized. Hence, the chances that a discriminatory promotion policy for blacks could be either implemented or maintained on any large scale are small. This in itself casts a shadow of doubt on the blocked-black-mobility argument as a viable alternative explanation.

If such discrimination existed, however, it could be detected by examining a rank distribution by race for the enlisted personnel of both services. Table 13 shows this rank-by-race distribution for Marine Corps enlisted personnel and prisoners. Although nonblack E9s slightly outnumber black E9s and black E1s slightly outnumber nonblack E1s, the rank distributions of blacks and nonblacks are remarkably similar. A large concentration of blacks in the lower ranks, which one would expect as a consequence of promotion discrimination, is not found in the Marine Corps data. Furthermore, it should be mentioned that the rank distributions of black and non-black prisoners indicate that both groups are drawn from the lower ranks: 85.80 percent of the nonblacks and 89.15 percent of the blacks rank E2 or below. These Marine Corps data, therefore, do not lend support to the hypothesis that discrimination exists with regard to the promotion of blacks.

Table 14 shows navy personnel and prisoners by rank and race. One notices immediately that the rank structure of the navy is some-what more middle heavy than the more even, bottom-heavy structure of the Marine Corps. These differences in rank structure reflect the aforementioned differences in job structure between the services. The navy depends for the most part on a large number of electronic and mechanical technicians whose required education and training place them in the E5 to E7 range (Department of the Navy 1972). Hence, unlike the Marine Corps which depends upon the E1–E3 infantrymen, the navy relies upon a large corps of middle-ranking technicians. It is, therefore, the presence of blacks and nonblacks in these middle ranks that is of greatest interest here.

As was the case in the Marine Corps, the discrepancies in rank between blacks and nonblacks are not great. In the crucial middle ranks, we find approximately equal proportions of blacks and non-blacks who rank E7 and E8, slightly more blacks rank E6, and slightly more nonblacks are at the E5 level. Thus, an examination of the technicians' ranks affords no evidence of large black-nonblack differences. Furthermore, when we group together nontechnicians (E3–E4) and seaman recruits (E1–E2), we find no significant differ-ence by race—58.24 percent of the nonblacks and 63.39 percent of the blacks fall into this E4-or-below category. It should also be noted that, like the Marine Corps, navy prisoners—regardless of race—tend to come from the lower ranks: 91.22 percent of the nonblacks and 96.57 percent of the blacks rank E3 or below.

The preceding discussion does not provide any substantial evidence that blacks are promoted at some rate that is very different from nonblacks. Therefore, the blocked-mobility argument, which

TABLE 13

Marine Corps Personnel and Prisoners by Rank and Race

| | Enlisted Personnel | | | | Prisoners | | | |
| | Non-Black | | Black | | Non-Black | | Black | |
Rank	Number	Percent	Number	Percent	Number	Percent	Number	Percent
E9	1,516	.98	70	.30	0	0.00	0	0.00
E8	3,373	2.18	234	1.02	0	0.00	0	0.00
E7	6,810	4.41	836	3.63	2	.16	0	0.00
E6	12,583	8.14	1,985	8.61	2	.16	0	0.00
E5	22,106	14.31	2,666	11.57	18	1.45	6	1.55
E4	22,845	14.79	2,293	9.95	47	3.79	5	1.29
E3	25,699	16.63	3,826	16.60	107	8.64	28	7.24
E2	30,322	19.62	4,757	20.64	210	16.95	84	21.71
E1	29,258	18.94	6,379	27.68	853	68.85	261	67.44
Unknown	0	0.00	0	0.00	0	0.00	3	.78
Total	154,512	100.00	23,046	100.00	1,239	100.00	387	100.00

Sources: Figures for enlisted personnel are adapted from Department of Defense 1972, vol. 1, p. 56. Figures for prisoners are compiled by the author.

TABLE 14

Navy Personnel and Prisoners by Rank and Race

Rank	Enlisted Personnel				Prisoners			
	Nonblack		Black		Nonblack		Black	
	Number	Percent	Number	Percent	Number	Percent	Number	Percent
E9	3,325	.70	79	.25	0	0.00	0	0.00
E8	8,655	1.81	315	1.00	0	0.00	0	0.00
E7	35,692	7.48	2,279	7.23	1	.14	0	0.00
E6	70,976	14.86	5,093	16.15	1	.14	0	0.00
E5	80,733	16.91	3,779	11.99	11	1.56	2	1.14
E4	109,271	22.88	3,818	12.11	45	6.37	2	1.14
E3	106,130	22.23	6,267	19.88	159	22.52	36	20.57
E2	45,026	9.43	6,326	20.06	195	27.62	77	44.00
E1	17,675	3.70	3,574	11.34	290	41.08	56	32.00
Unknown	0	0.00	0	0.00	4	.57	2	1.14
Total	477,483	100.00	31,530	100.00	706	100.00	175	100.00

Sources: Figures for enlisted personnel are adapted from Department of Defense 1972, vol. 1, p. 56. Figures for prisoners are compiled by the author.

41

relies largely on the notion that blacks are not equally promoted, breaks down. In concluding, then, the former explanation—emphasizing inconsistent education and authority statuses coupled with an unfavorable comparison level for alternatives—seems to best fit the data.

Three scholars, Moskos (1973) and Janowitz (1975) working in the military sociology and Stark (1972) working with the police, have suggested similar policies that would result in the reduction of discrimination for people in the age, rank, and education category just described. The policies focus on personnel recruitment and would require that position placement in the lower ranks be made solely on the basis of education and skill without consideration for time in the military or time in grade. Such a policy would have the effect of bringing level of responsibility more into line with skill and education, hence reducing the psychological and structural stresses previously described and bringing the opportunities available to older blacks with a high-school education more into line with those available to their white counterparts. It is interesting to note that officers in both the marines and navy are recruited in just this fashion. Extension of this program to the enlisted ranks would erase much of what discrimination still prevails there and would represent a large step toward eradicating problems of discrimination in the criminal-justice system of the sea services.

The two chapters that follow further assess the status of blacks and whites in the criminal-justice system with regard to offense patterns and relative sentence length. Since it has been established that once age, education, and pay grade are taken into account, black-white incarceration-rate differentials are minor, except in the high-education, low-rank, older-age-group category, we can begin to explore differentials in the characteristics of offenders and the kinds of crimes committed.

3

OFFENSE PATTERNS AND RACE
IN THE SEA SERVICES

For a great many years social scientists have studied and debated black-white differentials with regard to crime, particularly differences by race in arrest rate, adjudication, sentencing, and offense commission. Perhaps the longest running of these continuing issues, however, is that of race and offense: Do blacks in general commit more crimes than whites and, specifically, do blacks engage in violent crime more often than whites? Having already addressed crime differentials in Chapter 2, we will here focus concern on the types of offenses committed by blacks and whites in the navy and Marine Corps.

There are numerous difficulties in the analysis of offense statistics by race that require that any analysis of offense differentials be preceded by qualifiers (Bonger 1969; Dinitz and Reckless 1968; Guenther 1970; Nye, Short, and Olson 1958; Pettigrew 1975; Radzinowicz and Wolfgang 1971). From data on the civilian population, one is made sensitive to the fact that arrest data contain many problems, not the least of which is the idea that the reason for arrest may not necessarily correlate with whatever final charge might be levied. It is also known that arrests are by no means final and an offender may indeed be pronounced not guilty. Our analysis of incarceration data avoids many of the problems with data on arrests. This does not mean, of course, that incarceration data are flawless. However, remembering previous discussions of military-civilian criminal-justice systems, it can be argued that military incarceration data are certainly more useful for this kind of analysis than civilian data.

Who actually gets incarcerated in the civilian criminal-justice system is subject to several intervening variables that are operative to a much lesser extent in the military. Plea bargaining, rampant

in the civilian world, has a definite impact on which offenders make
it all the way to the "big house." The effect of this procedure is less
felt in the military due to more strict rules with respect to charging
a defendant and because of the relatively more precise definitions
of exactly what constitutes particular offenses (Department of Defense
1969). Also, variance in incarceration due to differential skill of
representing counsel is minimized in the military system. In most
cases involving enlisted personnel, counsel is provided; there is no
contest of who can afford to retain the more experienced or perhaps
"trickiest" lawyer. Thus, it is suggested that people incarcerated
in the military are not as select a group—sifted by income, race,
and social status—as people encountered in civilian institutions.

Finally, one additional selection process should be mentioned:
arrest—the point of first contact with the criminal-justice system.
Civilian data tell us that blacks have higher arrest rates than whites
(Tittle and Rowe 1974). It has been suggested, but not empirically
demonstrated, that the rate differential represents the policeman's
tendency to charge a black and simply reprimand a white, even under
very similar circumstances. While this explanation may not be
implausible, it should be noted that such a practice would be more
difficult to maintain in the military due to (1) the virtually complete
integration of the military police, (2) the relatively close surveillance
of military arresting officers by their superiors, and (3) the very
explicit conditions for arrest, which rarely permit warnings, and
their strict enforcement. Hence, while we must be aware of arrest
differentials that seem to select blacks more often then whites for
entrance into the criminal-justice system, it must be emphasized
that for military data the part of this differential that is due to overt
discrimination is probably quite small.

Having made the requisite qualifications, we can now turn
attention to analyses. The following section will focus on the
characteristics of offenders in the sea services rather than on rates
for particular offenses. This latter issue pertaining to the prevalence
of particular offenses will be assessed in subsequent sections on the
black violence hypothesis.

DISTRIBUTION OF OFFENSES IN THE NAVY
AND MARINE CORPS

A first look at the distribution of offenses in the sea services
provides an interesting contrast to offense patterns in the civilian
world. In the military, a hierarchically organized and basically
totalitarian institution, a major concern exists about the availability
and whereabouts of individual servicemen. All men perform a

TABLE 15

Absence without Leave versus All Other
Offenses, Navy and Marine Corps

Offense	Navy		Marine Corps	
	Number	Percent	Number	Percent
Absence without leave	609	69.13	1,125	69.19
All other offenses	203	23.04	405	24.91
Unknown	69	7.83	96	5.90
Total	881	100.00	1,626	100.00

Source: Compiled by the author.

function deemed necessary to the effective operation of the whole
body—failure to be present and performing one's function is seen as
a threat to the entire institution. Hence, military authorities view
unauthorized absence from one's post as an offense which, in the
event of mobilization, could hamper the unit's effectiveness and
ultimately take a toll in loss of life.

Table 15 indicates that this philosophy is rigidly enforced:
Nearly 70 percent of both navy and Marine Corps prisoners are
serving time for being absent without leave (AWOL). The near
equality of these figures also suggests that the AWOL rule is enforced
with similar zeal in both services. The fact that equal proportions
of prisoners are confined for AWOL should not, however, be permitted to mask the Marine Corps's higher relative rate for AWOL
offenses: 6.34 per 1,000 marines go AWOL while 1.21 per 1,000
sailors are AWOL.

Parenthetically, it is interesting to note that the navy is currently
considering decriminalizing AWOL offenses (Guthrie 1975). In these
times of economic instability, the logic for such a move is quite
compelling. It is expensive to maintain confinement facilities and
the men who are imprisoned contribute nothing in terms of work to
the service itself during their term of confinement. Hence, the
service loses considerably for each man confined. Much like the
reconsideration of marihuana smoking as a crime in the larger
society, military leaders are taking a careful look at AWOL. By
definition, men booked under this statute are not deserters and in
most cases they have not been absent for a long time period; many
AWOLs return of their own accord. It is argued that if AWOL is
decriminalized and handled under nonjudicial punishment, usually

involving pay forfeiture—the military equivalent of a fine—it will
permit deactivation of at least some incarceration facilities, increase
revenue through fines, increase overall effectiveness by keeping men
with their units, and boost morale by removing threat of incarceration for minor absences. The chances, therefore, are quite good
that AWOL will be decriminalized in the sea services in the near
future.

There are 134 articles and numerous subarticles in the Uniform
Code of Military Justice that specify criminal offenses in the American armed services. To attempt to examine all offenses would no
doubt prove to be a monumental—not to mention terribly confusing—
task. In November of 1972, the Task Force on the Administration
of Military Justice also faced this problem and, in response, developed
a classification scheme that placed all offenses in one of four groups:
(1) major military (or civilian) offenses, (2) confrontation or status
offenses, (3) unauthorized absences, and (4) other military offenses.
Figure 5 lists the specific offenses in the data at hand and the categories under which they were grouped. Offenses in class one are
most serious and meet one or more of the following criteria: (1) they
are offenses that must be tried by General Courts-Martial, (2) they
appear in the seven-offense, major-crime index devised by the
Federal Bureau of Investigation (1970, p. 5), (3) a sentence of death
or life imprisonment is a possible outcome. Class-two offenses are
largely peculiar to the military and involve defiance of constituted
authority with the additional condition that, if guilty, the offender
faces a sentence of confinement greater than 45 days or its equivalent.
Class-three offenses are also unauthorized absences. Together these
three offense classes group offenses into categories representing
issues of greatest concern to military leaders: serious crimes,
challenges of authority, and failure to perform one's duty due to an
unexcused absence. All three types represent the type of disruption
that potentially could severely hinder the operation of the military.
The fourth category, class four, represents an "all-other" category
composed of a very wide variety of offenses that are considered to
be less serious, less often charged, unspecified, and/or less threaten-
ing in terms of the three dimensions described above as vital to
preserving order in the military.

It is important to realize that no classification scheme can be
flawless and all such schemes introduce problems of lost detail.
It is, however, a cost that the analyst must pay in order to reduce
the analytic task to manageable, and interpretable, proportions.
Given these reservations, the scheme used here has the extra
advantage of reflecting issues of greatest relevance to the preserva-
tion of the military as an institution (see Andreski 1968). The following sections compare incidence of crime in these classes in the navy

FIGURE 5

Offense Classes Developed by the Task Force
on the Administration of Military Justice

Class 1. Major Military (or Civilian) Offenses

Murder	Manslaughter
Rape	Larceny
Robbery	Maiming
Arson	Assault
Burglary	Housebreaking

Class 2. Confrontation or Status Offenses

Disrespect, officer	Escape
Disobey, officer	Riot
Disobey orders	Assault, NCO*
Disobey, disrespect, NCO*	Provoking words, gestures

Class 3. Unauthorized Absence

AWOL	Desertion
Missing movement	

Class 4. Other Military (Civilian) Offenses

False official statements	Drunk driving
Malingering	Forgery
Sodomy	Extortion
Misbehavior as sentinal	Drunk on duty
Fraudulent claim	Unspecified
Destroy private property	Destroy government property
Maltreatment of subordinates	Perjury

*Noncommissioned officer.
Source: Department of Defense 1972.

and Marine Corps and focus on differentials by race, age, education, and pay grade.

Table 16 shows the distribution of navy and Marine Corps prisoners by offense class. As noted previously, the two services have about the same proportion of AWOL offenders and Table 16

TABLE 16

Offense Class by Service

Offense Class	Navy		Marine Corps	
	Number	Percent	Number	Percent
Major military offense	59	7.27	150	9.80
Confrontation or status offense	65	8.00	100	6.54
Unauthorized absence (AWOL)	609	75.00	1,125	73.53
Other military offense	79	9.73	155	10.13
Total	812	100.00	1,530	100.00

Source: Compiled by the author.

indicates that they also have about equal proportions of personnel confined under the "other military offense" catetory. There is a small discrepancy between the services, however, in the proportion of personnel confined under class-one and class-two offense categories. A greater proportion of Marine Corps offenders, 9.80 percent, are confined for major military offenses; only 7.27 percent of the navy prisoners were convicted of such offenses. Conversely, in the navy, 8.00 percent of the prisoners are in confinement for confrontation-of-status offenses, compared with 6.54 percent in the Marine Corps. In spite of these variations it has been pointed out

TABLE 17

Rates of Incarceration by Offense Class
and Service
(per thousand enlisted men)

Offense Class	Navy	Marine Corps
Major military offense	.12	.85
Confrontation or status offense	.13	.56
Unauthorized absence (AWOL)	1.21	6.34
Other military offense	.16	.87

Source: Compiled by the author.

that the magnitude of the service differences in basic categories are not great. For practical purposes it may be said that the proportional distribution of offenders in the navy and Marine Corps is equivalent (Department of Defense 1972; Goodspeed 1955). One should not lose sight, however, of the fact that while the four offense classes hold about the same proportion of offenders, the basic offense rate remains higher in the Marine Corps for all classes of offense (see Table 17).

Furthermore, the introduction of pay grade as a control does not radically alter the between-service comparison. For both services, personnel above the grade of E3 are less likely to be incarcerated. Sailors E3 or below are 25.75 times more likely to be incarcerated for an unauthorized-absence offense as navy prisoners above E3. Similarly, marine prisoners in or below E3 are 20.65 times as likely to commit an AWOL offense as marines above that grade.

Table 18 also shows that the proportion of personnel convicted of major military and confrontation or status offenses decreases as rank (pay grade) increases. Among navy personnel, men in the lower pay grades are 15.00 times more likely to be convicted of a major military offense as men in the higher pay grades. For the marines, lower-ranking men are 12.55 times as likely to be convicted of such offenses.

In general, men of lower rank have higher rates of conviction in all offense classes than men of higher rank. Furthermore, an exam-

TABLE 18

Convictions by Pay Grade and Service
(per thousand enlisted men)

Rank	Offense Class	Navy	Marine Corps
E1–E3	Major military offense	.30	1.38
	Confrontation or status offense	.34	.89
	Unauthorized absence (AWOL)	3.09	10.53
	Other military offense	.40	1.42
E4–E9	Major military offense	.02	.11
	Confrontation or status offense	.02	.12
	Unauthorized absence (AWOL)	.12	.51
	Other military offense	.02	1.00

Source: Compiled by the author.

ination of the proportion of persons convicted in the various offense classes indicates that the patterns described in Table 16 change only somewhat when pay grade is introduced into the analysis. Table 19 shows offense class by rank and service. Among both navy and Marine Corps prisoners, we see that most offenders were convicted of some unauthorized absence, without regard to rank of the offender. For major military and confrontation or status offenses, however, there is a change from the basic pattern. In the case of the navy, while the proportion of men convicted of confrontation offenses remains about the same for both rank categories, there is a higher proportion (10.53 percent) of men E4-E9 convicted of major military offenses (7.24 percent for E1-E3). The opposite is true for the Marine Corps, where about equal proportions of men are incarcerated for major military offenses but marines E4-E9 have proportionately twice as many convicted of confrontation offenses as is the case in the lower ranks.

TABLE 19

Offense Class by Rank and Service

Rank	Offense Class	Navy		Marine Corps	
		Number	Percent	Number	Percent
E1-E3	Major military offense	56	7.24	143	9.70
	Confrontation or status offense	63	8.14	92	6.24
	Unauthorized absence (AWOL)	580	74.94	1,092	74.08
	Other military offense	75	9.69	147	9.97
	Total	774	100.00	1,474	100.00
E4-E9	Major military offense	6	10.53	8	10.81
	Confrontation or status offense	5	8.77	9	12.16
	Unauthorized absence (AWOL)	39	68.42	38	51.35
	Other military offense	7	12.28	19	25.68
	Total	57	100.00	74	100.00

Source: Compiled by the author.

The increase in the proportion of major military offenses with increasing rank is only slight for both services and is probably due to the fact that age is not controlled. The doubling of the proportion of confrontation offenses among higher-ranking enlisted men in the Marine Corps is a function of the interaction of the kind of crimes in the offense category with the organization of the marines. To be convicted of disrespect or disobedience to an officer or of disobeying general orders, one must contact officers or be in a position to be receiving orders from officers. Unlike the navy, the Marine Corps is bottom heavy in that lower enlisted men regularly report to other enlisted men. Although aboard ship the captain and other officers have enlisted personnel (such as radio and sonar operators) who report directly to them, this is not usually the case in the marines. Hence, lower-ranking enlisted marines may only infrequently contact a commissioned officer directly and are thus less likely, from an organizational standpoint, to be charged with or convicted of a confrontation or status offense.

From previous analyses (see Chapter 2) we know that, in general, blacks have higher incarceration rates for all offenses than do whites. Table 20, which shows offense class by race and service, permits us to examine the relative distribution of black and white offenders across the four offense categories.

For both services and both races, the greatest proportion of offenders have been convicted of an unauthorized absence. Among navy prisoners, AWOL offenders account for 78.85 percent of the whites and 60.36 percent of the blacks. Unauthorized-absence offenders in the marines constitute 80.76 percent of white prisoners and 54.91 percent of the blacks. It is interesting to note that while AWOL is the modal offense category for all groups, white confinees in both services are more heavily represented in the unauthorized-absence class than blacks. Among navy prisoners the proportion of whites incarcerated for AWOL is 1.31 times the black proportion. The proportion of marine white AWOL offenders is 1.47 times the black proportion.

On the other hand, proportionately more black prisoners than white in both services have committed either major military or confrontation or status offenses. Slightly more than 20 percent of black navy prisoners, compared with less than 4 percent of the whites, are serving time for major military offenses. For the Marine Corps, 17.99 percent of the incarcerated whites and 6.62 percent of the blacks are in the major-military-offense category. These same differentials, although to a much lesser degree, appear when we look at confrontation or status offenses. Among navy prisoners, the proportion of blacks incarcerated for a confrontation offense is 1.24 times the white proportion; the proportion of black

TABLE 20

Offense Class by Race and Service

Offense Class	Navy White Number	Navy White Percent	Navy Black Number	Navy Black Percent	Marine Corps White Number	Marine Corps White Percent	Marine Corps Black Number	Marine Corps Black Percent
Major military offense	24	3.73	35	20.71	73	6.62	77	17.99
Confrontation or status offense	49	7.62	16	9.47	62	5.63	38	8.88
Unauthorized absence (AWOL)	507	78.85	102	60.36	890	80.76	235	54.91
Other military offense	63	9.80	16	9.47	77	6.99	78	18.22
Total	643	100.00	169	100.00	1,102	100.00	428	100.00

Source: Compiled by the author.

marine prisoners jailed for a confrontation offense is 1.58 times
the white proportion. While worthy of comment, the race differences
with respect to confrontation offenses are small relative to the
differentials for class-one and class-three offenses. Therefore,
the major patterns discernible in Table 20 are the overrepresentation
of white prisoners charged with AWOL offenses and the overrepresentation of black prisoners in major military offenses. What is perhaps
most striking about these differentials is their persistence when
controls for age and education are introduced.

Table 21 shows navy and Marine Corps prisoners by race,
offense class, and education. First, it should be mentioned that
our basic proportions do not change when education is taken into
account: AWOL still accounts for most offenders across services.
Furthermore, white confinees for unauthorized-absence offenses
persist in greater proportion than blacks across services and education groups. Also, the extent that whites outnumber blacks in this
category is remarkably stable. For navy prisoners, the proportion
of whites with less than a high-school education convicted of AWOL
is 1.32 times that of blacks; if they have a high-school diploma or
more, the proportion is 1.25 times that for blacks. Similarly, the
proportion of white marine confinees with less-than-high-school
training convicted of an unauthorized absence is 1.21 times that of
black marines with the same educational level. White marine
prisoners with a high-school education or more are serving AWOL
offenses in 1.27 times the proportion of their black counterparts.
The similarity of these white-black differentials across categories
of education and service emphasizes the stability of this finding.

The black overrepresentation in major military offenses also
persists when we introduce education into the analysis. In this case,
however, we find that in addition to the black-white differential, a
main effect for education is present in the navy data. For marine
prisoners with less than a high-school education, the black proportion
convicted of a major military offense is 3.12 times the white proportion. Black marine confinees with greater than a high-school
education are incarcerated for major military offenses proportionately
nearly three times as much as whites. The similarity of the magnitude of these ratios indicates that the black-white difference is
approximately the same for both educational groupings.

Looking at the same relationships for the navy prisoners, we
note a difference for the two levels of education. While the proportion of whites incarcerated for major military offenses is almost
the same for both categories of education, the proportion of blacks
increases by a factor of two when we move from the less-than-high-
school to the high-school-or-greater category. Thus, the conviction
differential (more blacks than whites) increases for those with a
high-school education or more.

TABLE 21

Offense Class by Race, Service, and Education

Race	Offense Class	Navy Less than High School		Navy High School or More		Marine Corps Less than High School		Marine Corps High School or More	
		Number	Percent	Number	Percent	Number	Percent	Number	Percent
White	Major military offense	14	4.22	10	3.23	45	5.56	29	8.36
	Confrontation or status offense	12	3.61	37	11.94	37	4.57	25	7.20
	Unauthorized absence (AWOL)	284	85.54	223	71.94	661	81.60	228	65.71
	Other military offense	22	6.63	40	12.90	67	8.27	65	18.73
	Total	332	100.00	310	100.00	810	100.00	347	100.00
Black	Major military offense	10	12.99	24	26.09	39	17.33	38	24.36
	Confrontation or status offense	6	7.79	10	10.87	22	9.78	15	9.62
	Unauthorized absence (AWOL)	50	64.94	53	57.61	152	67.56	81	51.92
	Other military offense	11	14.29	5	5.43	12	5.33	22	14.10
	Total	77	100.00	92	100.00	225	100.00	156	100.00

Source: Compiled by the author.

Table 22 shows that a control for age is not sufficient to remove the black-white differentials in class-one and class-three offenses. In general, as age increases, the proportion of personnel incarcerated for major military offenses decreases. However, the preponderance of blacks over whites in this offense category persists across age groups and services. Among navy prisoners, the proportion of blacks incarcerated for major military offenses in each age category is more than five times the white proportion. The magnitude of the differential is slightly smaller in the Marine Corps, but black prisoners still outnumber whites 3.85 to 1 in the young age group and 2.45 to 1 in the older category.

The overrepresentation of white offenders in the unauthorized-absence offense class also persists when age is controlled. It is interesting to note, though, that in the navy the proportion of white AWOL prisoners is about the same for both age groups while the proportion of black AWOL offenders increases from 55.93 percent in the young group to 75.00 percent among older sailors. Overall, however, the proportion of white prisoners who are AWOL is 1.44 times the black proportion among the 17-21 year olds and 1.03 times the black proportion in the 22-and-older group. Among marine prisoners the proportion of unauthorized-absence offenses decreases slightly as age increases for both racial groups. Even taking this into account, the ratio of whites to blacks still remains high in favor of whites.

Our analysis of offense patterns in terms of the task-force offense classes has yielded several interesting findings. First, the most common offense among incarcerated sailors and marines—without regard to race, pay grade, age, or education—is the unauthorized absence. Also, the incarceration rate for all offenses declines drastically for servicemen above the rank of E3; the basic proportions, heavy in AWOL, remain similar.

Further, with the introduction of race into the scheme, a strong black-white differential was detected for the major-military- and unauthorized-absence-offense classes. It was found that even when age, education, and pay grade were controlled, white prisoners proportionately outnumber blacks in the unauthorized-absence category and black confinees are disproportionately concentrated in the major-military-offense category. This finding holds for both the navy and the Marine Corps.

Given the nature of the crimes that compose the two offense classes, a tentative explanation for the race differential can be derived from the civilian literature on criminology. The major-military-offense category is composed largely of violent crimes (such as murder, rape, robbery, and assault), while the unauthorized-absence category is heavy with AWOLs—a comparatively nonviolent

TABLE 22

Offense Class by Race, Service, and Age

Race	Offense Class	Navy				Marine Corps			
		17-21		22 and Older		17-21		22 and Older	
		Number	Percent	Number	Percent	Number	Percent	Number	Percent
White	Major military offense	18	4.35	6	2.67	41	5.58	32	7.57
	Confrontation or status offense	23	5.56	26	11.56	42	5.71	20	4.73
	Unauthorized absence (AWOL)	333	80.43	174	77.33	586	79.73	304	71.87
	Other military offense	40	9.66	19	8.44	66	8.98	67	15.84
	Total	414	100.00	225	100.00	735	100.00	423	100.00
Black	Major military offense	28	23.73	7	14.58	43	21.50	34	18.58
	Confrontation or status offense	13	11.02	3	6.25	14	7.00	24	13.11
	Unauthorized absence (AWOL)	66	55.93	36	75.00	129	64.50	106	57.92
	Other military offense	11	9.32	2	4.17	14	7.00	19	10.38
	Total	118	100.00	48	100.00	200	100.00	183	100.00

Source: Compiled by the author.

and, in terms of the psychological literature, escapist crime. The tendency of blacks to be arrested and incarcerated for violent crimes more frequently than whites is an empirical regularity in the literature on crime (Forslund 1970; Wolfgang and Cohen 1970). Hence, what we are probably picking up in our analysis is this violent-nonviolent crime differential by race. The black violence hypothesis that we have invoked as an explanation introduces several additional issues. If the hypothesis is correct, offense categories constructed to reflect violent and nonviolent crimes should exhibit a very pronounced race differential. Furthermore, we can begin to examine, in light of military data, some of the theoretical claims regarding the relationships among black violence, education, and general social status. Thus, in the following section our concern shifts from the population of offenders and their characteristics to a concern with the rate or frequency with which navy and Marine Corps personnel commit violent offenses.

BLACK VIOLENCE IN THE SEA SERVICES

Initially it should be mentioned that violence is not an easy or particularly "clean" concept with which to deal. Volumes have been written on the subject and arguments still persist regarding exactly how violence and crime mesh. Marvin Wolfgang (1975, p. 3), a veteran of the National Commission on the Causes and Prevention of Violence, recalls:

Violence is a term we struggled a great deal with in the violence commission. Essentially we spoke of it as an infliction of injury on the body or property of others. But this is certainly not a completely satisfying, totally comprehensive definition. We know that there are crimes of violence and these were easily handled by our definition. But there are other kinds of violence that deal with violence on the highways; there is legitimized violence by people in legitimate authority . . . there is political violence . . . [and] . . . the gnawing at infants' toes by rats in the ghettos may be viewed as a form of violence.

Like the violence commission, we shall here recognize the myriad forms that violence may take and opt for a similar operationalization. For the purpose of the present analysis, violent offenses shall be those that involve bodily injury or attack upon another human being. Nonviolent offenses are ones that do not involve attack or physical injury.

This definition of violence departs only slightly from the commission's in that we do not treat assaults on property as violent crimes. There are several reasons behind this omission. Burglars are known to shun violence and/or contacts with their victims (Robertson 1974). Carrying a weapon or attacking a homeowner is a poor risk for the burglar. In the first place contact increases the probability of apprehension and, further, if indicted, burglary carries a much lighter sentence alone as opposed to the case where assault or murder are also included in the charges. Thus, burglary as an occupation is qualitatively distinct from other crimes that we have included among the violent offenses and, as such, will be included as a nonviolent offense.

Property-damage offenses are omitted from the violent-crime category due to many peculiar circumstances that often accompany charges of destruction of property in the military. Personnel in the sea services are usually "signed out" or responsible for equipment that they use in everyday work. Hence, personnel are signed out for jeeps, radio equipment, sonar scopes, aircraft, and similar sorts of items. Further, even a low-level (E3 or E4) noncommissioned officer (NCO) may be responsible for equipment used by his subordinates. If some damage is incurred on such equipment, however, both the subordinate and the NCO are likely to be prosecuted on charges of property destruction. Therefore, in the military, people incarcerated for property destruction may fall into either category: they could have physically destroyed property—a violent offense—or they could have been responsible for property that was destroyed—a nonviolent offense. Unfortunately there is no way, given the present data, to separate these two kinds of offenders. Hence, the category is neither clearly violent nor clearly nonviolent and will be omitted altogether from the analysis.

The offenses grouped as violent crimes are shown in Figure 6. It will be noticed that a number of offenses that were present in Figure 5 have been eliminated altogether from the present scheme. The crimes omitted are largely from the confrontation category (disrespect, disobedience, provoking words and gestures). Most omissions were made on the grounds that the offense in question did not clearly fall into either a violent or nonviolent category. Also, in the case of some offenses, like provoking words or gestures and disrespect, there is the additional difficulty of possible selective enforcement due to selective perception or to differing definitions of what is provoking or disrespectful. In an effort to make the present analysis as clean-cut as possible, such questionable offenses were eliminated from consideration.

Table 23 shows the black and white rates of incarceration for violent offenses by service. These data show a pronounced race

FIGURE 6

Offenses Grouped as Violent Crimes

Murder	Manslaughter
Rape	Robbery
Assault	Assault, NCO
Riot	Disorderly (misbehavior)
Maltreatment of subordinates	

Source: Compiled by the author.

differential for both services: Blacks in the navy are 18.17 times more likely than whites to commit a violent offense and Marine Corps blacks are incarcerated for violent offenses 6.83 times as often as whites. Aside from the general observation that the violent crime rate for both races is higher in the marines than the navy, we also see that Table 23 confirms that a race-violence relationship exists at the zero-order level in both services.

As mentioned in Chapter 1, there has been much debate among social scientists regarding why this race differential exists. Sociologists generally believe that the difference is a function of black versus white social environments. There are, however, two schools of thought regarding the analysis of black violence as a function of the environment in which blacks operate. The first line of reasoning emphasizes the nature of the environment at the moment; hence, concern here is with the nature of the present stimulus environment of offenders. Such reasoning is adhered to by those who support the subculture-of-violence thesis (Wolfgang 1958; Wolfgang and

TABLE 23

Violent Offenses by Race and Service
(per thousand enlisted men)

Service	White	Black
Navy	.06	1.09
Marine Corps	.36	2.46

Source: Compiled by the author.

Ferracuti 1967). It is argued that within the subculture, "various stimuli such as a jostle, a slightly derogatory remark, or the appearance of a weapon in the hands of an adversary are perceived differently than in the dominant culture" (Erlanger 1975, p. 280); in the subculture such stimuli evoke a violent reaction. Thus, concern is with the "toughness" of the environment at hand and with the required "tough" responses to that environment (Miller 1958). Therefore, it is among those who live in the tough environment— young, male, white and nonwhite lower-class adults—that "we should find in most intense degree a subculture of violence" (Wolfgang and Ferracuti 1967, p. 153). It is this logic that leads us to predict that general social status—age, education, and income—if controlled adequately, would destroy the race differential with reference to violent crime. If the reasoning is correct, people of the same social status experience the same milieu and should be equally represented with regard to violence.

The second school of thought regarding the role of the environment represents a difference in degree rather than in kind. Espoused for the most part by social scientists with a social-psychological or developmental orientation, this argument acknowledges that the immediate environment plays a vital role in human behavior but suggests that the environment in which the individual was socialized is of paramount importance for understanding behavior (Akers 1964; Bandura 1969; Bandura and Walters 1963; Gewirtz 1969; Kunkel 1970; McCandless 1969). It is from this perspective that it is argued that:

> the circumstances of Whites and Negroes are not fully
> comparable, that the [early socialization] experience
> of the Negro in America differs not only in degree but
> in kind from that of lower class White ethnic minorities
> (Green 1970, pp. 476-77).

Therefore, even under conditions of similar socioeconomic status, we should not expect the racial differential in violent crime to disappear (Johnson 1941; Moses 1947; Pettigrew 1964).

Several attempts have been made since the early 1940s to test these two lines of reasoning on civilian data. Most such studies have found that where the control for social status is introduced, the black-white differential does not disappear (Akers 1964; Johnson 1941; Moses 1947; Nye, Short, and Olson 1958; Wolfgang and Cohen 1970). Critics have pointed out, however, that it is difficult to obtain a reliable measure of social status because, at least in the civilian world, black people and white people, even with similar age, education, and income, can have very different life-styles.

Indeed, the social milieu of a white who makes 20,000 dollars annually may not even resemble that of a black with the same salary.

As previously indicated, the military data, due to certain peculiar organizational features of military life, offer the opportunity to introduce a more refined control for social-status variables than is possible with civilian data. Hence, when simultaneous controls for pay grade, education, and age are made, we have groups of blacks and whites who definitely (1) have about the same income, (2) have about the same level of supervisory responsibility, (3) are of similar age and educational level, and (4) probably live in similar kinds of on-base housing. A closer matching on social status would be diffi-cult to achieve. In this fashion we can begin to examine the behavior of the black-white differential in military data when social status is controlled.

Table 24 shows navy violent crime rates by race, education, pay grade, and age. Initially it should be emphasized that where there are sufficient cases to make a comparison, the black violence rates are higher than the white rates. Further, this observation holds across all categories of age, education, and rank.

Education seems to have a moderating effect on violence at both age levels and rank levels. As education level increases, the violent crime rate for both blacks and whites decreases. Interestingly, among black and white sailors ranking E2 and below, as age increases so does the rate of violent offenses. This finding is consistent with the conclusions drawn from Chapter 2 where it was argued that older,

TABLE 24

Navy Violent Offenses by Race, Education,
Pay Grade, and Age
(per thousand enlisted personnel)

| | | E1-E2 | | E3 and Higher | |
		Less than High School	High School	Less than High School	High School
17-21	White	.18	.03	.83	.21
	Black	1.84	1.17	12.66	3.52
22 and	White	.41	.26	.09	.02
older	Black	2.48	2.05	—*	—

*Too few cases for meaningful estimate of rate.
Source: Compiled by the author.

low-ranking sailors, whether black or white, constituted the most problematic group in terms of the incidence of crime. Thus, both racial groups show similar patterns across age, education, and rank.

The violent crime rates for the Marine Corps on the same variables is shown in Table 25. Once again we find that across all categories of the control variables, the violent crime rate for blacks is almost always at least a factor of three larger than the white rate. The education effects seen in the navy data are also present for the Marine Corps: For all levels of age and rank, the violent crime rates of both blacks and whites decreases as education increases. Table 25 also indicates that in general and for both races, as rank increases the violent crime rate decreases. With respect to age, among marines ranking E2 or lower and within both categories of education, as age increases so does the violent crime rate. Again, this finding is consistent with the navy data and highlights the older members of the low-ranking group as more problematic with regard to military criminal justice.

With the descriptive task completed, we can turn attention to black-white differentials in violent crime across the various control variables. Table 26 shows the ratios of the black violent crime rate to the white rate by service, age, education, and rank. Thus, the figures in the table indicate, figuratively, how many blacks are incarcerated for violent offenses for each white (per 1,000 enlisted men) within the various categories of control variables. It should be emphasized at the outset that across all categories for both services, the black violent crime rate is at least twice as high as

TABLE 25

Marine Corps Violent Offenses by Race,
Education, Pay Grade, and Age
(per thousand enlisted men)

| | | E1-E2 | | E3 and Higher | |
		Less than High School	High School	Less than High School	High School
17-21	White	.65	.08	.39	.08
	Black	2.33	1.48	4.72	.99
22 and	White	2.57	.88	.73	.10
older	Black	7.76	5.12	1.64	.75

Source: Compiled by the author.

TABLE 26

Ratios of Black to White Violent Crime Rates
by Service, Age, Education, and Pay Grade

| Service | Age | E1–E2 | | E3 and Higher | |
		Less than High School	High School or More	Less than High School	High School or More
Navy	17–21	10.22	39.00	15.25	16.76
	22 and older	5.00	9.54	–*	–
Marines	17–21	3.58	18.50	12.10	33.00
	22 and older	3.27	5.82	2.25	7.50

*Insufficient cases to form a ratio.

Source: Compiled by the author.

the white rate. Furthermore, for both the navy and the Marine Corps, the black-white differential (with blacks having the higher rate) increases with education and decreases with age. Therefore, while the black violence continues to be higher than the white rate, increasing age moderates the differential (shrinks the gap) and increasing education extends the differential. With reference to the aforementioned argument regarding controls for general social status, then, the important point to be derived from Table 26 is that the black-white differential in violent crime does persist. Furthermore, the black rate remains substantially higher than the white rate in all categories of the social-status controls.

In summary, our findings do not lend support to the argument that blacks and whites of similar social status have similar rates for the commission of violent offenses. Since this is the case, indirect support is afforded the argument that the basic socialization of blacks and whites is fundamentally different and, in later adult life, these differences persist even if other social factors are held constant. To fully examine this hypothesis would go far beyond the scope of the present data. At best, the data at hand are sufficient to vitiate the social-status argument and to suggest that the socialization approach, pending further empirical analyses, is the next most powerful alternative explanation for the black-white violent-crime differential detected here.

4

BLACKS, WHITES, AND SENTENCING

Sentencing occupies a central position in the administration of criminal justice both in the military and civilian systems. Thus, there has been much concern, especially in the civilian world, that sentences be assigned based on the circumstances and nature of the offense and offender—ascribed characteristics of the offender, such as race, should have no impact on the punishment. There has been some controversy in the civilian literature over the extent to which sentences vary by race of the offender.

While lacking much real agreement on exactly who seems to be most discriminated against on which types of offenses, the literature does document the fact that sentence disparities do exist. Thorsten Sellin, in an early study comparing sentences among natural-born whites, foreign-born whites, and blacks, reported numerous though unsystematic differences that he suggested could be accounted for by "the human equation in judicial administration" (1935, p. 217). More recently, Edward Green has summarized the empirical quandry presented by studies of race differentials in sentencing:

> The research evidence on which the charge of discrimina-
> tion is grounded is equivocal in that some studies show
> a general tendency on the part of the court to impose
> heavier penalties on Negroes in comparison with Whites,
> while others show that for most offenses Negroes receive
> lighter sentences (1964, p. 348).

Several scholars have speculated that the absence of a consistent pattern in sentence differentials—even when controls for factors such as type of offense, prior record, socioeconomic factors, and number of offenses are introduced—indicates that the characteristics of the

offender are less vital in understanding sentence differences than
are the characteristics of the sentencer (Bullock 1961, p. 417;
Elkin 1957; Guenther 1970). Thus, in reviewing sentencing as
practiced in Canada and the United States, John Hogarth points out
that:

> The imposition of unequal sentences for the same offense,
> or for offenses of comparable seriousness, without a
> clearly visible justification, amounts, in the public mind,
> to judicial caprice. Accused and counsel openly "jockey"
> for lenient judges and the notion that the criminal justice
> system is fairly and evenly applied is thereby shown to
> be a myth (1971, p. 6).

These arguments add a new dimension to the analysis of sentence
differentials and suggest that the logic for analysis used in the
studies that have generated the existing inconclusive and contradictory
literature is flawed. Studies produced to date assume that variance
in sentencing is wholly or, at least, mostly due to differing characteristics of offenders and that characteristics of the sentencer or
of the sentencing process do not introduce additional variance.
Hence, control variables have been primarily characteristics of
offenders. Indeed, the fact that this assumption is incorrect is
supported by the disagreement and failure to identify patterns in
the research literature of the past 30 years. In defense of the
research, however, it must be said that scholars were not ignorant
and were in fact aware of the incorrectness of the assumption. In
the report of the President's Commission on Law Enforcement and
the Administration of Justice, Mr. Justice Jackson (then attorney
general) noted that "it is obviously repugnant . . . that judgement
meted out to an offender should depend in large part on . . . the
personality of the particular judge before whom the case happens
to come for disposition" (1967, p. 144). The very practical problem
this circumstance produces for researchers—that of "controlling"
for judge—is extremely difficult to implement in the civilian system.
To examine the idea that variation in sentence length is largely a
function of the sentencer, a system wherein the rules for sentencing
are explicit and evenly applied is necessary. The criminal-justice
system of the sea services provides just such an atmosphere.

As noted in Chapter 1, the conduct of courts-martial and civilian
trials differ in a number of respects. One major difference is with
regard to sentencing. Courts-martial are not always, in fact are
infrequently, presided over by a military judge. Thus, the role of
sentencer is played alternately by unit commanders, their adjutants,
or whomever is assigned by the senior convening officer to head the

board of officers constituting the court-martial. The impact of this practice is that the sentencer role is not embodied in a single individual continuously over time and most officers pronouncing sentence have perhaps done so only a few times in their careers. This rotating of the sentencer function forces those fulfilling the role, if for no other reason than due to lack of familiarity with the rules, to pay careful attention to the Manual for Courts-Martial. This in itself has a standardizing effect on the process of sentencing.

Furthermore, the Uniform Code of Military Justice (UCMJ) appears as Chapter 47 of the Manual of Courts-Martial. The UCMJ, under article 127, section C-6(A), lists a very long item called the Table of Maximum Punishments. This table lists all offenses with which military personnel may be charged and provides, in columns, the kinds of punishments that may be administered and the maximum confinement specified in years and months to which guilty offenders may be sentenced. While in the civilian system a judge would see such a table as an encroachment upon his legitimate right to administer justice, there is evidence that in the military the table is seen as a valuable guide by sentencers (Special Civilian Committee for the Study of the United States Army Confinement System, 1970, p. 101-07). Therefore an unusual degree of standardization is built into the sentencing process in the military through written guides and through the rotation of sentencers, which encourages reliance on the written guides. If our arguments are correct and much of the variation in civilian sentencing is a function of variance in the sentencing process (that is, between judges' decision-making processes), then, in the more standardized atmosphere of the military system, a control for offense class should be all that is necessary to make any differentials in sentence length between blacks and whites disappear.

The following sections, then, will focus on the question of black-white differences in sentence length among navy and Marine Corps offenders. Essentially, three issues will be presented: race and presentence confinement, comparative sentence lengths, and offenders with prior records.

PRESENTENCE CONFINEMENT

Presentence confinement in the sea services is a reasonably common phenomenon that should not be confused with pretrial confinement. Presentence confinees have been tried, pronounced guilty, and assigned a sentence by the court but are in confinement prior to the official start of the sentence. Presentence confinement may occur for a variety of reasons: (1) the defendant may be awaiting appeal, (2) if sentenced by a Summary Court-Martial, he may have

requested and be awaiting a review of his sentence by a military
review board, (3) he may be awaiting transfer to different confinement facilities where he will begin to serve his assigned sentence
upon arrival, or (4) he may be awaiting the official start of his
sentence due to paper-work delays in signing the offender out of his
unit and into a confinement facility.

It would seem that if discrimination against blacks were likely
at any stage of the military criminal-justice system, the presentence
confinement phase would be the more likely spot since officials could,
if they chose, "drag their feet" to differentially extend the confinement period with the lowest probability of detection. Further, such
discrimination would be low risk if detected since it could be blamed
on the slowness of paper work; red tape is widespread in a bureaucracy the size of the military and could legitimately be used as a
scapegoat.

Interestingly, there is virtually no black-white differential with
respect to presentence confinement. Table 27 shows the sentence
status of navy and Marine Corps prisoners by race. For both services, the proportions of blacks and whites in each sentence status
are almost identical. Of white navy prisoners, 42.77 percent have
a sentence and 57.23 percent are presentence. For black sailors,
57.40 percent are presentence. The percentage difference between
whites and blacks, 0.17 percent is negligible.

The same situation prevails for Marine Corp prisoners. Sentenced white marines account for 59.62 percent of the prisoners;
the remaining 40.38 percent are presentence. The black-white

TABLE 27

Navy and Marine Corps Prisoners by
Sentence Status and Race

Service	Sentence Status	White		Black	
		Number	Percent	Number	Percent
Navy	Sentence	281	42.77	72	42.60
	Presentence	376	57.23	97	57.40
	Total	657	100.00	169	100.00
Marine Corps	Sentence	694	59.62	233	60.21
	Presentence	470	40.38	154	39.79
	Total	1,164	100.00	387	100.00

Source: Compiled by the author.

TABLE 28

Presentence Navy and Marine Corps
Prisoners by Offense Class

Offense Class	Navy		Marine Corps	
	Number	Percent	Number	Percent
Major military offense	31	6.55	55	8.81
Confrontation or status offense	23	4.86	22	3.53
Unauthorized absence	391	82.66	493	79.01
Other military offense	28	5.92	54	8.65
Total	473	100.00	624	100.00

Source: Compiled by the author.

difference in the Marine Corps amounts to only 0.59 of one percentage point.

It is interesting to note also that proportionately more navy prisoners than marines are in presentence confinement. However, as Table 28 shows, the proportions of presentence prisoners confined under the four offense categories follow the same pattern found in earlier analyses of prisoners with a sentence: heaviest in the unauthorized-absence category, followed by major military offenses, with smaller proportions in each of the two remaining offense classes. Since this pattern holds for both services, it is reasonable to suggest that prisoners with a presentence status simply reflect the same general characteristics of prisoners with a sentence status. Most important, though, is the observation that black and white offenders are equally represented in the presentence category.

RACE AND SENTENCE LENGTH

It was initially argued that variation in sentence length is probably more a function of variation in the sentencer than of variation in offenders. This hypothesis was suggested after a review of the research introducing controls for various offender characteristics revealed no consistent pattern in sentence lengths. It was suggested that the military criminal-justice system provided a setting that minimized variation in the sentencing process and, therefore, a control for offense type should be sufficient to erase any black-white differential in sentence length in the data.

Table 29 shows navy and Marine Corps prisoners by sentence length, race, and offense class. It will immediately be noticed that the proportions of blacks and whites in each sentence category by offense class are very similar. Indeed, even though the marines offer slightly longer sentences than the navy for all categories except major military offenses, the proportions of blacks and whites remain about equal for both services.

Table 30 shows the ratios of black to white prisoners in each category of service, sentence, and offense class. A ratio of 1.00 indicates that exactly the same proportion of blacks and whites occupy the category. In all 19 cells where there are enough cases to form a stable ratio, we find that the values hover close to unity. This indicates that with only small variation, black and white offenders in both services receive approximately the same sentence within classes of offense. Furthermore, we can assess this variation statistically by examining differences in mean sentence length. Table 31 shows mean sentence length by service, offense class, and race, and provides a t-test of the difference of mean sentence length between white and black prisoners. An examination of the t-value column reaffirms our conclusion from the tabular analysis: None of the black-white differences in mean sentence length are even remotely close to statistical significance. Thus, the present data indicate that when offense type is controlled, blacks and whites receive approximately identical sentences. The slight variation that does show up is not statistically reliable.

Up to this point, little has been said about offenders with prior records. The reasoning behind this omission was mentioned in Chapter 1, where it was noted that offenders in the military with prior records have some interesting characteristics not common to civilian offenders with prior records. Due to the stipulation that military personnel convicted of serious offenses be discharged after serving their sentence, we know that people with prior records have convictions only for nonserious offenses. We therefore expect that, first, there are not many military offenders who have priors and, second, that there are not any great differences between first offenders and those with previous records.

Of all navy prisoners, 13.96 percent have prior records. Breaking down priors by race, we find that the proportion of black offenders with previous records (14.45 percent) is about the same as the proportion for white offenders (13.64 percent). Marine Corps prisoners show a slightly higher overall proportion of 22.63 percent with prior records, but the black-white difference remains minor:

TABLE 29

Navy and Marine Corps Prisoners by Sentence Length, Race, and Offense Class

Service	Sentence	Major Military Offense				Confrontation or Status Offense				Unauthorized Absence Offense				Other Military Offense			
		White		Black		White		Black		White		Black		White		Black	
		Number	Percent	Number	Percent	Number	Percent	Number	Percent	Number	Percent	Number	Percent	Number	Percent	Number	Percent
Navy	1-3 months	5	29.41	4	30.77	15	47.88	9	69.23	140	72.16	25	69.44	20	54.05	5	50.00
	4-6 months	3	17.65	3	23.08	13	39.63	2	15.38	39	20.10	9	25.00	8	21.62	3	30.00
	7+ months	9	52.94	6	46.15	4	12.50	2	15.38	15	7.73	2	5.56	9	24.33	2	20.00
	Total	17	100.00	13	100.00	32	100.00	13	100.00	194	100.00	36	100.00	37	100.00	10	100.00
Marine Corps	1-3 months	22	40.74	12	28.57	21	43.75	16	51.61	270	54.11	82	58.57	26	27.96	3	15.79
	4-6 months	10	18.52	7	16.67	10	20.83	9	29.03	149	29.86	32	22.86	17	18.28	3	15.79
	7+ months	22	40.74	23	54.76	17	35.42	6	19.36	80	16.03	26	18.57	50	53.76	13	68.42
	Total	54	100.00	42	100.00	48	100.00	31	100.00	499	100.00	140	100.00	93	100.00	19	100.00

Source: Compiled by the author.

TABLE 30

Ratios Black to White Prisoners by Service, Sentence Length, and Offense Class

Service	Sentence	Major Military Offense	Confrontation or Status Offense	Unauthorized Absence	Other Military Offense
Navy	1-3 months	1.05	1.45	.96	.94
	4-6 months	1.31	—*	1.24	1.34
	7+ months	.88	1.23	—	—
Marine Corps	1-3 months	.70	1.18	1.08	—
	4-6 months	.90	1.33	.77	.87
	7+ months	1.34	—	1.16	1.27

*Insufficient cases to form a ratio.

Source: Compiled by the author.

72

TABLE 31

Mean Sentence Length by Service, Offense Class, and Race

Service	Offense Class	White[a]	Black[a]	t value[b]	df
Navy	Major military offense	14.64 (17)	10.69 (13)	.501[c]	28
	Confrontation or status offense	6.09 (32)	5.15 (13)	.588[c]	43
	Unauthorized absence	3.80 (194)	2.97 (36)	1.850[d]	228
	Other military offense	9.13 (37)	8.30 (10)	.160[c]	45
Marine Corps	Major military offense	25.71 (54)	25.14 (42)	.047[c]	94
	Confrontation or status offense	7.58 (48)	4.80 (31)	1.870[d]	77
	Unauthorized absence	4.43 (499)	5.07 (140)	.927[c]	637
	Other military offense	21.09 (93)	28.63 (19)	.747[c]	110

[a]Number of cases given in parentheses.
[b]Difference of $\bar{x}$.
[c]Not significant, $.5 > p > .1$.
[d]Not significant, $.1 > p > .05$.
Source: Compiled by the author.

20.93 percent of black marine offenders have priors and 23.16 percent of the white offenders have previous offenses on their record.

Furthermore, the offense patterns of black and white prisoners with prior records are similar to the patterns of first offenders in both services. Table 32 shows prisoners with a sentence by service, offense class, race, and prior record. It should be mentioned that offenders of both races who have prior records are slightly more heavily represented in the unauthorized-absence category than first offenders. This is probably a function of the fact that AWOL is a common prior offense (men get jailed but not discharged for it) and military offenders who go AWOL once unsuccessfully will usually try again (Department of Defense 1972, vol. 2, pp. 69-74). Thus,

TABLE 32

Prisoners with Sentence by Service, Offense Class, Race, and Prior Record

Service	Offense Class	No Prior Record				Prior Record			
		White		Black		White		Black	
		Number	Percent	Number	Percent	Number	Percent	Number	Percent
Navy	Major military offense	12	6.59	11	23.40	5	5.10	2	8.00
	Confrontation or status offense	29	15.93	7	14.89	3	3.06	6	24.00
	Unauthorized absence	115	63.19	20	42.55	79	80.61	16	64.00
	Other military offense	26	14.29	9	19.15	11	11.22	1	4.00
	Total	182	100.00	47	100.00	98	100.00	25	100.00
Marine Corps	Major military offense	47	11.55	35	23.18	7	2.44	7	8.64
	Confrontation or status offense	31	7.62	23	15.23	17	5.92	8	9.88
	Unauthorized absence	263	64.62	79	52.32	236	82.23	61	75.31
	Other military offense	66	16.22	14	9.27	27	9.41	5	6.17
	Total	407	100.00	151	100.00	287	100.00	81	100.00

Source: Compiled by the author.

the military tends to build up a body of AWOL offenders with prior
AWOL charges on their records. Given this logic, it comes as no
surprise that (adding across race) 80 percent of all offenders with
prior records in both services are currently serving time for an
unauthorized absence.

Tables 33 and 34 show sentence length, offense class, and race
for navy and Marine Corps prisoners broken down by prior record.
An important initial observation is that the basic equality in sentence
length between black and white prisoners still holds for first offenders
in the navy. Unfortunately, among prisoners with a prior record
there are sufficient cases to make comparisons only in the
unauthorized-absence offense class. In both services, the other
three offense categories contain so few cases that meaningful analyses
are impossible. For unauthorized-absence offenders we again find
virtually no proportionate differences between blacks and whites
in sentence length. In all sentence categories that have data, there
is only a small black-white differential across both navy and Marine
Corps offenders with prior records.

Further, it should be emphasized that sorting out prisoners
with prior records does not change the basic black-white sentence-
length equality among first offenders. Table 35 shows the ratios
of black to white first offenders by service, sentence length, and
offense class. Although removal of offenders with prior records
has decreased the number of cases and thereby the number of
comparable ratios that can be formed, the remaining ratios still
hover very near unity. This finding indicates that as we found before
sorting out priors, within offense classes in both the navy and
marines, black and white prisoners show no major differentials
with regard to sentence length.

RACE AND SENTENCING: SUMMARY
AND CONCLUSIONS

Contrary to the civilian research on race differentials in
sentence length, which shows varying differentials for different
offense classes, our analysis of military data shows no significant
black-white sentence differential in any of the four offense classes.
Also, black and white prisoners remained represented in equal
proportions in the sentence categories when offenders with prior
records were separated out.

It was argued that the more standardized sentencing process
in the military—that is, the fact that the criteria for sentence length
are more evenly applied and less subject to variation between
sentencers—would produce greater equality of sentence length among

TABLE 33

Navy Prisoners by Offense Class, Sentence Length, Race, and Prior Record

Offense Class	Sentence	No Prior Record				Prior Record			
		White		Black		White		Black	
		Number	Percent	Number	Percent	Number	Percent	Number	Percent
Major military offense	1–3 months	4	33.30	4	36.40	0	0.00	0	0.00
	4–6 months	3	25.00	2	18.20	1	20.00	1	50.00
	7+ months	5	41.70	5	45.40	4	80.00	1	50.00
	Total	12	100.00	11	100.00	5	100.00	2	100.00
Confrontation of status offense	1–3 months	14	48.30	4	57.10	1	33.33	5	83.33
	4–6 months	13	44.80	2	28.60	0	0.00	0	0.00
	7+ months	2	6.90	1	14.30	2	66.67	1	16.67
	Total	29	100.00	7	100.00	3	100.00	6	100.00
Unauthorized absence	1–3 months	90	78.30	14	70.00	50	63.30	11	68.80
	4–6 months	20	17.40	4	20.00	19	24.10	5	31.20
	7+ months	5	4.30	2	10.00	10	12.60	0	0.00
	Total	115	100.00	20	100.00	79	100.00	16	100.00
Other military offense	1–3 months	14	53.80	5	55.60	6	54.50	0	0.00
	4–6 months	6	23.10	3	33.30	2	18.20	0	0.00
	7+ months	6	23.10	1	11.10	3	27.30	1	100.00
	Total	26	100.00	9	100.00	11	100.00	1	100.00

Source: Compiled by the author.

TABLE 34

Marine Corps Prisoners by Offense Class, Sentence Length, Race, and Prior Record

Offense Class	Sentence	No Prior Record				Prior Record			
		White		Black		White		Black	
		Number	Percent	Number	Percent	Number	Percent	Number	Percent
Major military offense	1–3 months	18	38.30	9	25.70	4	57.10	3	42.90
	4–6 months	8	17.00	6	17.10	2	28.60	1	14.20
	7+ months	21	44.70	20	57.20	1	14.30	3	42.90
	Total	47	100.00	35	100.00	7	100.00	7	100.00
Confrontation or status offense	1–3 months	11	35.50	10	43.50	10	58.80	6	75.00
	4–6 months	5	16.10	7	30.40	5	29.40	2	25.00
	7+ months	15	48.40	6	26.10	2	11.80	0	0.00
	Total	31	100.00	23	100.00	17	100.00	8	100.00
Unauthorized absence	1–3 months	135	51.30	50	63.30	135	57.20	32	52.50
	4–6 months	66	25.10	11	13.90	83	35.30	21	34.40
	7+ months	62	23.60	18	22.80	18	7.60	8	13.10
	Total	263	100.00	79	100.00	236	100.00	61	100.00
Other military offense	1–3 months	12	18.18	1	7.10	14	51.90	2	40.00
	4–6 months	9	13.64	3	21.40	8	29.60	0	0.00
	7+ months	45	68.18	10	71.40	5	18.50	3	60.00
	Total	66	100.00	14	100.00	27	100.00	5	100.00

Source: Compiled by the author.

TABLE 35

Ratios of Black to White Prisoners with No Prior Record by Service, Sentence Length, and Offense Class

Service	Sentence	Major Military Offense	Confrontation or Status Offense	Unauthorized Absence	Other Military Offense
Navy	1-3 months	1.09	1.18	1.12	1.03
	4-6 months	.77	—*	1.15	—
	7+ months	1.09	—	—	—
Marine Corps	1-3 months	.68	1.23	1.24	—
	4-6 months	1.01	1.88	.76	—
	7+ months	1.28	—	.97	—

*Insufficient cases to form a ratio.

Source: Compiled by the author.

78

offenders in general. Under such a system, any departure from the
normative procedure associated with race would be readily visible
since, if black offenders were the object of systematic discrimination, their pattern of sentences would consistently clash with that
of white offenders across all offense classes. This, however, is
not the case. Therefore, the failure to find any sentence differential
supports our earlier contention that offenders, once inside the military
criminal-justice system, are treated in like fashion without regard
to ascribed statuses (for example, race) and largely differentiated
only on the basis of offense type.

5

DISCRIMINATION AND
MILITARY CRIMINAL JUSTICE

In the short space of 25 years, the navy and Marine Corps have undergone a transformation from completely segregated to completely integrated institutions. Although the changes have been uneven and not without stress, it should be emphasized that the military has implemented integration to a greater extent in these 25 years than the larger society has managed in over 100 years.

The major focus of this research has been to determine the extent to which service-wide integration has also meant equal treatment for black and white members of the sea services. We have sought to answer this question specifically with regard to criminal justice in the military. Our investigation involved careful review of data regarding all phases of contact with the system. In comparing blacks with whites, we examined both the frequency and outcomes of courts-martial, rates of confinement, types of offenses, and sentence lengths and other punishments. The central findings from our scrutiny of each of these issues are summarized in this chapter. It should be mentioned at the outset, however, that remarkably little evidence of institutionalized differential treatment was found.

With respect to incarceration rates, it was determined that once differences in age, education, and rank were taken into account, black rates were only slightly higher than those for whites. Indeed, whether black or white, the greatest proportion of prisoners, both in the navy and Marine Corps, have similar background characteristics: they are 17-21 years of age, rank E3 or lower, and have less than a high-school education. In general the black-white differential in confinement is especially small throughout the Marine Corps and for navy personnel who rank E4 or higher.

The only exception to this rule of general equality of incarceration rates occurs for the same category of personnel in both services.

Blacks in the lowest rank classification, above the age of 22 with a high-school education or more have an incarceration rate nearly two times greater than the rate for their white counterparts. This discrepancy was explained by appealing to a labeling-theory argument and by noting the differential opportunities available to blacks and whites with these demographic characteristics. The older, low-ranking, but higher-educated soldier or sailor operates in a high-stress environment where his activities are closely monitored. Hence, blacks and whites with these attributes have a higher probability of at least short-term incarceration than other personnel; circularity is built in to the extent that repeated offenses result in even closer surveillance, further increasing the chances of having even minor infractions of the rules detected. The higher incarceration rate for blacks in this category is related to greater numbers of blacks with these characteristics who remain in the service. It was noted that while older, educated, but low-ranking whites have better opportunities in the civilian world than in the military, the outlook for black personnel is quite different. For blacks the cost of escaping this stress in the service is probably outweighed by the greater relative discrimination in the civilian world, which is accompanied by generally lower levels of remuneration and job security. What appears to be the point of greatest discrimination with regard to incarceration, then, is more a function of structural variables than of systemic discrimination at an individual level. This single large differential should not, however, be permitted to obscure the major point: Where age, education, and rank are the same, blacks and whites have very similar incarceration rates. This strongly suggests that, in the navy and Marine Corps, the important differentiating factors among confinees are largely those other than race.

In reviewing the offense patterns of navy and Marine Corps confinees, the most striking finding was that 70 percent of all the offenders had been incarcerated as a result of some type of unauthorized absence. Furthermore, there seemed to be a split by race among AWOL offenders. That is, most unauthorized absences were attributable to young, low-ranking, white personnel, and this appeared to be true for both services. Blacks, on the other hand, were most heavily represented in the category of major military offenses. Hence, whites seem to dominate the particular class of offense for which most confinees in the sea services are imprisoned. Aside from this obvious conclusion, it is important to attempt to understand why whites seem predisposed to going AWOL and blacks appear to disproportionately commit major military crimes.

A closer examination of these apparent racial differentials revealed the more general finding that relative to whites, blacks

are more often incarcerated for violent crimes. This racial differential by violence has been discovered previously in studies of
offense patterns among civilian offenders, but it is generally believed
that the relationship between race and violence is artificial; if we
compare offenders of the same social status, blacks and whites
should be equally violent. Thus, based on these arguments derived
from the civilian literature, it was hypothesized that controls for
general social status—age, education, and pay grade—would vitiate
the difference in violent crime rate between blacks and whites. This,
however, turned out not to be true. Even with the controls for general
social status, the black violence rate remained in all cases a minimum
of twice as high as the white violent crime rate. Therefore, the
subculture-of-violence thesis, predicated on the argument that among
certain classes the tendency toward violence is higher whether one
is black or white, is not supported by our analysis of the military
data. Indeed, among military personnel, where a control for social
status produces very homogeneous groups of blacks and whites in
terms of their current social environment, the preponderance of
black violent offenders persists at nearly the same level as was the
case without controls. The persistence of the black-white differential
in spite of controls tends to support the socialization-based argument
that there are fundamental differences—cultural, social, and
psychological—in the way lower-status blacks and whites are socialized
and that these differences persist even if the later life circumstances
of the individuals are similar. In support of this logic, Barth (1961)
has noted that the language patterns of poor blacks are distinct from
those of poor whites and remain so in spite of limited socioeconomic
mobility that may occur in the lives of the blacks. The idea here is
that a distinct set of behavior patterns socialized during childhood
and adolescence tend to persist although the environment may change.
Thus, the world view of lower-socioeconomic-status blacks and
whites—the way they interpret and act upon stimuli—are basically
different. It is suggested here that one aspect of this difference,
in addition to the language considerations just mentioned, is the
tendency of blacks to react with what whites perceive as violence
in numerous stimulus situations.

Our analysis of prisoners' sentence lengths yielded the interesting
conclusion that once type of offense is taken into account, there are
no statistically significant black-white differences with regard to
length of sentence. This finding stands in sharp contrast to the confused and contradictory literature on civilian sentencing that affords
no consistent pattern of evidence. In explaining our finding of no
race differential, it was suggested that a major problem with civilian
studies of sentencing lies in the fact that although extensive controls
are used for characteristics of the offender, there are virtually no

controls for characteristics of the sentencer. Furthermore, a review
of the legal literature cues one to the fact that in the civilian world,
considerable between-judge variation in sentencing criteria and practices exists. We suggested in Chapter 4 that in a setting where
sentencer variation is minimized or at least routinized, what appear
to be unsystematic differences between blacks and whites would not
persist. In the military criminal-justice system, it was argued that
sentencing criteria and their application are characterized by a high
degree of standardization. This condition is a function of (1) the fact
that the sentencer role is rotated and not embodied in any single
person over a long time period and (2) the great detail in which sentences for offenses are prescribed. This standardized sentencing
atmosphere and the official policy of nondiscrimination in the sea
services appear to be responsible for our failure to find any significant differences in sentence length for blacks and whites within types
of offenses.

Our study of the treatment of blacks and whites in the criminal-
justice system of the navy and Marine Corps has uncovered virtually
no evidence of institutionalized discrimination against either racial
group. This is not to say, of course, that no discrimination exists
and that whites and blacks live side by side in complete harmony.
One can always expect that some whites and some blacks, on an
individual level, will engage in discriminatory practices. It is to
be emphasized, however, that no institutional or systematic discrimination of important magnitude was detected here. The instances
of differential treatment that were uncovered were found to be for the
most part a function of interactive peculiarities of the military and
civilian sectors. For example, our finding that low-ranking, older,
better-educated blacks have a high relative incarceration rate due
to their high representation in the service but remain in the military
for its more equalitarian atmosphere and better work opportunities,
serves as convincing testimony to the better relative racial treatment in the sea services (see also Yarmolinsky 1971, pp. 343-45).

In conclusion, our data indicate that the application of criminal
justice in the sea services is remarkably even with respect to race.
This is particularly ironic in view of the fact that many servicemen,
social scientists, and citizens have long speculated that the military
is a bastion of white power and traditionalism and that blacks tend
to suffer in such an institution. Perhaps, as Charles Moskos (1973,
p. 106) notes, on the level of interpersonal relations and/or in times
of compulsory military service, such charges may carry an element
of truth. It remains, however, that the aggregate data do not provide
evidence of any systematic discrimination policies operating with
regard to criminal justice. The question of the extent to which this
absence of discrimination pervades other aspects of the sea services

is beyond the scope of the data at hand. It is probably safe to assume, however, that antidiscrimination policies have been pursued with equal zeal in most areas of military life. If this is indeed the case, then we cannot but concur with Professor Moskos who argues that "if American society is ever to realize its democratic promise, the direction it ought to take in race relations will most likely have been set by its men and women in military uniform" (1973, p. 106).

Akers, Ronald. 1964. "Socioeconomic Status and Delinquent Behavior." Journal of Research in Crime and Delinquency 1 (January): 38-46.

Andreski, Stanislav. 1968. Military Organization and Society. Berkeley: University of California Press.

Arnold, David. 1970. The Sociology of Subcultures. Berkeley, Calif.: Glendessary Press.

Bandura, Albert. 1969. Principles of Behavior Modification. New York: Holt, Rinehart and Winston.

Bandura, Albert, and Walters, Richard. 1963. Social Learning and Personality Development. New York: Holt, Rinehart and Winston.

Barth, E. A. T. 1961. "The Language Behavior of Negroes and Whites." Pacific Sociological Review 4 (Fall): 69-72.

Barth, E. A. T., and Noel, Donald. 1972. "Conceptual Frameworks for the Analysis of Race Relations." Social Forces 50 (March): 333-48.

Bidwell, Charles. 1961. "The Young Professional in the Army." American Sociological Review 26 (June): 360-72.

Blalock, Hubert. 1967. Toward a Theory of Minority-Group Relations. New York: John Wiley and Sons.

_____. 1972. Social Statistics. New York: McGraw-Hill.

Block, Herbert, and Flynn, Frank. 1956. Delinquency. New York: Random House.

Blumenthal, M.; Kahn, R.; Andrews, F.; and Head, K. 1972. Justifying Violence: Attitudes of American Men. Ann Arbor, Mich.: Institute for Social Research.

Bonger, Willem A. 1969. Race and Crime. Montclair, N.J.:
Patterson Smith.

Boskin, Joseph. 1969. Urban Racial Violence in the Twentieth
Century. Beverly Hills, Calif.: Glencoe Press.

Briggs, D. L. 1958. "Behavioral Inadequacies among Naval
Recruits." Military Medicine 123: 449-53.

Brodsky, Stanley, and Eggleston, Norman. 1970. The Military
Prison: Theory, Research and Practice. Carbondale: Southern
Illinois University Press.

Brodsky, Stanley, and Komaridis, G. 1966. "Military Prisonization."
Military Police Journal 15: 8-19.

____. 1968. "Self-disclosure in Prisoners." Psychological
Reports 23: 403-07.

Bross, I. O. J. 1958. "How to Use Rigit Analysis." Biometrics
14: 18-38.

Bullock, Henry. 1961. "Significance of the Racial Factor in the
Length of Prison Sentences." Journal of Criminal Law,
Criminology and Police Science 52: 411-17.

Campbell, John. 1813. Naval History of Great Britain. London:
John Stockdale, Piccadilly.

Canter, F. M., and Canter, A. N. 1957. "Authoritarian Attitudes
and Adjustment in a Military Situation." United States Armed
Forces Medical Journal 8: 1201-07.

Chambliss, William. 1974. "The State, the Law and the Definition
of Behavior as Criminal or Delinquent." In Handbook of
Criminology, edited by Daniel Glaser. Chicago: Rand McNally.

Chappell, Duncan, and Monahan, John. 1975. Violence and Criminal
Justice. Lexington, Mass.: D. C. Heath and Company.

Chappell, R. A. 1945. "Naval Offenders and Their Treatment."
Federal Probation 9: 3-7.

Claver, S. 1954. Under the Lash: A History of Corporal Punishment in the British Armed Forces. London: Torchstream.

Clinard, Marshall B. 1963. Sociology of Deviant Behavior. New
    York: Holt, Rinehart and Winston.

Coates, C. H., and Pellegrin, R. J. 1965. Military Sociology.
    University Park, Md.: Social Science Press.

Craige, John. 1941. The Marines. New York: W. W. Norton.

Cressey, Donald. 1961. The Prison: Studies in Institutional and
    Organizational Change. New York: Holt, Rinehart and Winston.

Cressey, Donald and Ward, David. 1969. Delinquency, Crime,
    and Social Process. New York: Harper and Row.

Davies, James. 1970. "Violence and Aggression: Inmate or Not?"
    Western Political Quarterly 23: 611-23.

Demaris, Ovid. 1971. America the Violent. Baltimore: Penguin
    Books.

Department of Defense. 1969. Manual for Courts-Martial, United
    States. Rev. ed. Washington, D.C.: Government Printing
    Office.

_____. 1972. Report of the Task Force on the Administration of
    Military Justice in the Armed Forces. 4 vols. Washington,
    D.C.: Government Printing Office.

Department of the Army. 1974. A Pictorial Tour of Black America:
    Past and Present. Philadelphia: United Publishing Corporation.

Department of the Navy. 1968. History of U.S. Marine Corps
    Operations in World War II. Washington, D.C.: Government
    Printing Office.

_____. 1972. Enlisted Minority Recruitment Guide: Navy Personnel
    15152. Washington, D.C.: Government Printing Office.

_____. 1972. Semi-Annual Statistical Report: Navy-Marine Corps
    Prisoners. Washington, D.C.: Government Printing Office.

Deutch, Martin; Katz, Irwin; and Jensen, Arthur. 1968. Social
    Class, Race and Psychological Development. New York: Holt,
    Rinehart and Winston.

Dinitz, Simon, and Reckless, Walter C. 1968. Critical Issues in the Study of Crime. Boston: Little, Brown and Company.

Duff, D. F., and Arthur, R. J. 1967. "Between Two Worlds: Filipinos in the U.S. Navy." American Journal of Psychiatry 123: 838-43.

Elkin, Winifred. 1957. The English Penal System. Baltimore: Penguin Books.

Erickson, M. 1969. "Military Injustice." Playboy 66 (June): 70-71.

Erlanger, Howard. 1975. "The Empirical Status of the Subculture of Violence Thesis." Social Problems 21: 280-92.

Federal Bureau of Investigation. 1970. Crime in the United States: Uniform Crime Reports. Washington, D.C.: Government Printing Office.

Forslund, Morris. 1970. "A Comparison of Negro and White Crime Rates." Journal of Criminal Law, Criminology and Police Science 61 (June): 96-102.

French, Elizabeth, and Ernest, Raymond. 1955. "The Relation between Authoritarianism and Acceptance of Military Ideology." Journal of Personality 24 (December): 181-91.

Frodi, Ann. 1974. "On Elicitation and Control of Aggressive Behavior." Goteborg Psychological Reports 4: 1-16.

Geis, Gilbert. 1965. "Statistics Concerning Race and Crime." Crime and Delinquency 11 (April): 61-69.

Gewirtz, Jacob. 1969. "Mechanisms of Social Learning: Some Roles of Stimulation and Behavior in Early Human Development." In Handbook of Socialization Theory and Research, edited by D. Goslin. Chicago: Rand McNally.

Glaser, Daniel. 1946. "The Sentiments of American Soldiers Abroad toward Europeans." American Journal of Sociology 51-433-38.

_____. 1974. Handbook of Criminology. Chicago: Rand McNally.

Gluckman, Max. 1965. Politics, Law and Ritual in Tribal Society. New York: Mentor Books.

Goodspeed, W. K. 1955. "The Unsuitable Enlisted Seaman."
United States Armed Forces Medical Journal 6: 244-48.

Goslin, David. 1969. Handbook of Socialization Theory and
Research. Chicago: Rand McNally.

Graham, H. D., and Gurr, T. R. 1969. The History of Violence
in America. New York: Bantam Books.

Green, Edward. 1964. "Inter- and Intra-racial Crime Relative to
Sentencing." Journal of Criminal Law, Criminology and Police
Science 55: 348-58.

_____. 1970. "Race, Social Status and Criminal Arrest." American
Sociological Review 35: 376-90.

Gross, Llewellyn. 1966. Sociological Theory. New York: Harper
and Row.

Guenther, Anthony. 1970. Criminal Behavior and Social Systems.
Chicago: Rand McNally.

Guthrie, E. R. 1975. Personal communication. Affiliated, Office
of Naval Research. Department of the Navy. Washington, D.C.

Hagan, John. 1975. "Law, Order and Sentencing: A Study of
Attitude in Action." Sociometry 38: 374-84.

Hakeem, M. 1946. "Armed Forces and Criminality." Journal of
Criminal Law and Criminology 37: 120-31.

Hall, E. T. 1947. "Race Prejudice and Negro-White Relations in
the Army." American Journal of Sociology 52: 401-09.

Hankoff, L. D. 1959. "Interaction Patterns among Military Prison
Personnel." United States Armed Forces Medical Journal
10: 1416-27.

Harlow, Harry, and Woolsey, Clinton. 1968. Biological and
Biochemical Bases of Behavior. Madison: University of
Wisconsin Press.

Henry, Andrew and Short, James. 1954. Suicide and Homicide:
Some Economic, Sociological and Psychological Aspects of
Aggression. Glencoe, Ill.: Free Press.

Henshel, Richard. 1970. "Military Correctional Objectives:
    Social Theory, Official Policy and Practice." In The Military
    Prison, edited by S. Brodsky and N. Eggleston. Carbondale:
    Southern Illinois University Press.

Hogarth, John. 1971. Sentencing as a Human Process. Toronto:
    University of Toronto Press.

Huie, W. B. 1954. The Execution of Private Slovik. Boston:
    Little, Brown and Company.

Janowitz, Morris. 1960. The Professional Soldier. New York:
    Free Press.

_____. 1964. The New Military: Changing Patterns of Organization.
    New York: Russell Sage Foundation.

_____. 1975. "The All-Volunteer Military as a Sociopolitical
    Problem." Social Problems 22 (February): 432-49.

Janowitz, Morris, and Little, Roger. 1965. Sociology and the
    Military Establishment. New York: Russell Sage Foundation.

Johnson, Guy B. 1941. "The Negro and Crime." The Annals
    217: 93-104.

Johnson, Roger. 1972. Aggression in Man and Animals. Phila-
    delphia: W. B. Saunders and Company.

Jones, Terry. 1974. "Institutional Racism in the United States."
    Social Work 19 (March): 218-25.

Klineberg, Otto. 1935. Race Differences. New York: Harper
    and Brothers.

Knox, Dudley. 1936. A History of the United States Navy. New
    York: G. P. Putnam.

Knudten, Richard D. 1968. Criminological Controversies. New
    York: Appleton-Century-Crofts.

Korn, Richard, and McCorkle, L. W. 1960. Criminology and
    Penology. New York: Holt, Rinehart and Winston.

Kourvetaris, George. 1971. "The Role of the Military in Greek
    Politics." International Review of History and Political Science
    8 (August): 91-114.

Kunkel, John. 1970. Society and Economic Growth. New York:
    Oxford University Press.

Lee, U. G. 1966. The Employment of Negro Troops in World
    War II. Washington, D.C.: Office of the Chief of Military
    History, Department of the Army.

Lewis, M. M. 1960. A Social History of the Navy, 1793-1815.
    London: George Allen and Union.

Little, Roger. 1971. Handbook of Military Institutions. Beverly
    Hills, Calif.: Sage Publications.

Locke, B.; Cornsweet, A. C.; Bromberg, W.; and Apuzzo, A. A.
    1945. "A Study of 1063 Naval Offenders." United States Navy
    Medical Bulletin 44: 73-86.

Lorenz, Konrad. 1969. On Aggression. New York: Bantam Books.

McCandless, Boyd. 1969. "Childhood Socialization." In Handbook
    of Socialization Theory and Research, ed. D. Goslin. Chicago:
    Rand McNally.

Mack, Raymond W. 1958. Race, Class and Power. New York:
    Van Nostrand Reinhold Company.

Mandelbaum, D. G. 1952. Soldier Groups and Negro Soldiers.
    Berkeley: University of California Press.

Matza, David. 1969. Becoming Deviant. Englewood Cliffs, N.J.:
    Prentice-Hall.

Meier, August, and Rudwick, Elliot. 1969. "Black Violence in
    the 20th Century: A Study in Rhetoric and Retaliation." In
    The History of Violence in America, edited by H. Graham and
    T. Gurr. New York: Bantam Books.

Miller, Kent, and Dreger, R. M. 1973. Comparative Studies of
    Blacks and Whites in the United States. New York: Seminar
    Press.

Miller, Walter. 1958. "Lower Class Culture as a Generating
Milieu of Gang Delinquency." Journal of Social Issues 14
(Summer): 5-19.

Moses, Earl. 1947. "Differentials in Crime Rate between Negroes
and Whites, Based on Comparisons of Four Socioeconomically
Equated Areas." American Sociological Review 12: 411-20.

Moskos, Charles. 1966. "Racial Integration in the Armed Forces."
American Journal of Sociology 72 (September): 132-48.

_____. 1970. The American Enlisted Man: The Rank and File in
Today's Military. New York: Russell Sage Foundation.

_____. 1971. Public Opinion and the Military Establishment.
Beverly Hills, Calif.: Sage Publications.

_____. 1972. "The Social Equivalent of Military Service." Teachers
College Record 73 (September): 7-12.

_____. 1973. "The American Dilemma in Uniform: Race in the
Armed Forces." The Annals 406: 106.

_____. 1974. "The Concept of the Military-Industrial Complex."
Social Problems 21 (April): 498-512.

Mueller, W. R. 1945. "The Negro in the Navy." Social Forces
24: 110-15.

Mulvihill, Donald, and Tumin, Melvin. 1969. Crimes of Violence:
A Staff Report Submitted to the National Commission on the
Causes and Prevention of Violence. Washington, D.C.:
Government Printing Office.

Nelson, D. D. 1956. The Integration of the Negro into the U.S.
Navy. New York: Farrar, Straus and Young.

Northrup, Herbert, and Jenkins, Frank. 1974. Minority Recruiting
in the Navy and Marine Corps. Philadelphia: Wharton School,
University of Pennsylvania.

Nuttin, Joseph, and Greenwald, Anthony. 1968. Reward and
Punishment in Human Learning. New York: Academic Press.

Nye, F. Ivan; Short, James; and Olson, Virgil. 1958. "Socio-economic Status and Delinquent Behavior." American Journal of Sociology 63: 381-89.

Peck, William. 1975. Personal communication. Affiliated, United States Navy Bureau of Personnel. Law Enforcement and Corrections Division.

Pettigrew, Thomas. 1964. A Profile of the American Negro. Princeton, N.J.: D. Van Nostrand Company.

_____. 1975. Racial Discrimination in the United States. New York: Harper and Row.

Pettigrew, Thomas, and Spier, R. B. 1962. "The Ecological Structure of Negro Homicide." American Journal of Sociology 67: 621-29.

Pratt, Fletcher. 1941. The Navy: A History. New York: Garden City Publishing.

President's Commission on Law Enforcement and the Administration of Justice. 1967. The Challenge of Crime in a Free Society. Washington, D.C.: Government Printing Office.

Quinney, Richard. 1970. The Social Reality of Crime. Boston: Little, Brown and Company.

Radzinowincz, Leon, and Wolfgang, Marvin. 1971. Crime and Justice. 3 vols. New York: Basic Books.

Reasons, Charles, and Kuykendall, Jack. 1972. Race, Crime, and Justice. Pacific Palisades, Calif.: Goodyear Publishing Company.

Richardson, S.; Dohrenwend, B.; and Klein, D. 1965. Interviewing: Its Form and Functions. New York: Basic Books.

Robertson, John. 1974. Rough Justice: Perspectives on Lower Criminal Courts. Boston: Little, Brown and Company.

Sarkesian, Sam C. 1972. The Military-Industrial Complex. Beverly Hills, Calif.: Sage Publications.

Savitz, Leonard. 1967. Dilemmas in Criminology. New York: McGraw-Hill.

Schafer, Stephen. 1969. Theories in Criminology. New York: Random House.

Scheflen, Kenneth C. 1975. Personal communication. Assistant Director for Analysis. Department of Defense. Manpower Research and Data Analysis Center. Alexandria, Virginia.

Schlesinger, Arthur, Jr. 1968. Violence: America in the Sixties. New York: Signet Books.

Schrag, Clarence. 1966. "Elements of Theoretical Analysis in Sociology." In Sociological Theory: Inquiries and Paradigms, edited by L. Gross. New York: Harper and Row.

Schur, Edwin. 1968. Law and Society: A Sociological View. New York: Random House.

Secretary of Defense. 1975. Annual Defense Department Reports. Washington, D.C.: Government Printing Office.

Secretary of the Navy. 1897. Annual Report to the President for the Year 1897. Washington, D.C.: Government Printing Office.

Sellin, Thorsten. 1935. "Race Prejudice in the Administration of Justice." American Journal of Sociology 41 (September): 212-17.

Sellin, Thorsten and Wolfgang, Marvin. 1964. The Measurement of Delinquency. New York: John Wiley and Sons.

Siberman, Charles. 1964. Crisis in Black and White. New York: Random House.

Singer, R. G., and Shaw, C. C. 1957. "The Passive-Aggressive Personality." United States Armed Forces Medical Journal 8: 62-69.

Sjoberg, Gideon, and Nett, Roger. 1967. A Methodology for Social Research. New York: Harper and Row.

Skinner, Emmett W. 1945. "The Navy's Correctional Program." Prison World 7: 8-30.

Special Civilian Committee for the Study of the U.S. Army Confine-
    ment System. 1970. Report. Washington, D.C.: Government
    Printing Office.

Spencer, J. C. 1954. Crime and the Services. London: Routledge
    and Kegan Paul.

Stark, Rodney. 1972. Police Riots: Collective Violence and Law
    Enforcement. Belmont, Calif.: Wadsworth.

_____. 1973. Society Today. Delmar, Calif.: CRM Books.

_____. 1975. Social Problems. New York: Random House.

Stark, Rodney, and Cohen, Larry. 1974. "Discriminatory Labeling
    and the Five-Finger Discount: An Empirical Analysis of Differ-
    ential Shoplifting Dispositions." Journal of Research in Crime
    and Delinquency 11: 25-39.

Stark, Rodney, and Erlanger, Howard. 1972. The Establishment
    Militants. Berkeley: Survey Research Center, University of
    California.

Stark, Rodney, and McEvoy, James. 1970. "Middle Class Violence."
    Psychology Today 4: 52-54.

Stillman, Richard. 1968. Integration of the Negro into the United
    States Armed Forces. New York: Praeger.

Stouffer, S.; Suchman, E.; DeVinney, E.; Starr, S.; and Williams, R.
    1949. The American Soldier: Adjustment during Army Life.
    Princeton: Princeton University Press.

Street, David. 1965. "The Inmate Group in Custodial and Treat-
    ment Settings." American Sociological Review 30: 40-55.

Sutherland, Edwin, and Cressey, Donald. 1960. Principles of
    Criminology. New York: Lippincott.

Terry, Robert. 1967. "Discrimination in the Handling of Juvenile
    Offenders by Social Control Agencies." Journal of Research
    in Crime and Delinquency 4: 218-30.

Thomas, Pat; Thomas, Edmund; and Ward, Samuel. 1974. Percep-
    tions of Discrimination in Non-judicial Punishment. San Diego:
    Navy Personnel Research and Development Center.

Thorne, F. C. 1953. "The Frustration-Anger-Hostility States:
A New Diagnostic Classification." Journal of Clinical Psychology
9: 334-39.

Tittle, C. R., and Rowe, Alan. 1974. "Certainty of Arrest and
Crime Rates: A Further Test of the Deterrence Hypothesis."
Social Forces 52 (June): 455-62.

U.S. Congress, House. 1973. Armed Services Committee. Report
of the Special Subcommittee on Disciplinary Problems in the
United States Navy. 93rd Cong., 2nd sess., H.A.S.C. 92-81.

Van den Berghe, Pierre. 1967. Race and Racism: A Comparative
Perspective. New York: John Wiley and Sons.

Vander Zanden, James W. 1966. American Minority Relations:
The Sociology of Race and Ethnic Groups. New York: Ronald
Press.

Vinson, T., and Homel, R. 1975. "Crime and Disadvantage."
The British Journal of Criminology 15 (January): 21-31.

Weil, F. E. G. 1947. "The Negro in the Armed Forces." Social
Forces 26: 95-98.

Wolfgang, Marvin. 1958. Patterns of Criminal Homicide. Philadelphia: University of Pennsylvania Press.

_____. 1975. "Contemporary Perspectives on Violence." In
Violence and Criminal Justice, edited by D. Chappell and
J. Monahan. Lexington, Mass.: Lexington Books.

Wolfgang, Marvin, and Cohen, Bernard. 1970. Crime and Race.
New York: Institute of Human Relations Press.

Wolfgang, Marvin, and Ferracuti, Franco. 1967. The Subculture
of Violence: Towards an Integrated Theory in Criminology.
London: Tavistock Social Science Paperbacks.

Yarmolinsky, Adam. 1971. The Military Establishment. New
York: Harper and Row.

Zald, Mayer. 1962. "Organizational Control Structures in Five
Correctional Institutions." American Journal of Sociology
68: 335-45.

Zurcher, Louis. 1965. "The Sailor Aboard Ship." Social Forces
    43 (March): 389–400.

Stark, Rodney, 2-3, 42
stockades, 4

Table of Maximum Punishments,
    67
Task Force on the Administration
    of Military Justice, 46
Truman, President Harry S.,
    14-15, 17

unauthorized absences:
    decriminalization of, 45-46;
    frequency of, 45-46; on prior
    record, 73; by race, 55-57
Uniform Code of Military Justice:
    articles of, 46; introduction
    to, 5; and sentence length, 67

violence: concept of, 57-58;
    effect of education on, 61-62;
    in Marine Corps, 59; in navy,
    59; by race, 58-64; and
    socialization, 64; social psy-
    chology of, 60-61, 62-64;
    subculture of, 59-60

Wolfgang, Marvin, 57, 59-60
World War I: and de facto
    segregation, 16; general, 16;
    and military justice, 33
World War II: general, 16;
    Marine Corps policy during,
    17; navy policy during, 16-17

Zumwalt, Elmo, 1

RONALD W. PERRY is Assistant Professor of Sociology and Senior Systems Analyst with the Institute for Social Research at the University of Hartford in West Hartford, Connecticut. He spent three years as a researcher at Battelle Memorial Institute in Seattle, Washington, and has taught at Arizona State University, the University of Washington, and Pacific Lutheran University.

Dr. Perry has published numerous papers in the areas of social psychology, social movements, complex organizations, and the philosophy of science. He is coauthor of Organizational Response to Changing Community Systems (Kent State University Press, 1976).

Professor Perry holds a B.S. and A.M. from Arizona State University and the Ph.D. from the University of Washington.

BARGAINING FOR JUSTICE: Case Disposition and
Reform in the Criminal Courts

Suzann R. Thomas Buckle and
Leonard G. Buckle

THE EFFECTIVENESS OF CORRECTIONAL
TREATMENT: A Survey of Treatment Evaluation
Studies

Douglas Lipton, Robert Martinson,
and Judith Wilks

CRIME PREVENTION AND SOCIAL CONTROL

edited by Ronald L. Akers
and Edward Sagarin